Is There a Father in the House?

Preparing Spiritual Sons to Lead the Church

Is There a Father in the House?

Preparing Spiritual Sons to Lead the Church

Paul Bersche

© Copyright 1995 — Paul Bersche

All rights reserved. This book is protected under the copyright laws of the United States of America. This book may not be copied or reprinted for commercial gain or profit. Short quotations or occasional page copying for personal or group study is permitted and encouraged. Permission will be granted upon request. Unless otherwise identified, Scripture quotations are from the New American Standard version of the Bible, ©1960, 1962, 1963, 1968, 1971, 1973, 1975, 1977 by The Lockman Foundation. Used by Permission. Scriptures marked (KJV) are from the King James Version of the Bible. Emphasis within Scripture is the author's own

Take note that the name satan and related names are not capitalized. We choose not to acknowledge him, even to the point of violating grammatical rules.

Treasure House
a division of
Destiny Image
P.O. Box 310
Shippensburg, PA 17257-0310

ISBN 1-56043-834-7

For Worldwide Distribution
Printed in the U.S.A.

Destiny Image books are available through these fine distributors outside the United States:

Christian Growth, Inc.,
Jalan Kilang-Timor, Singapore 0315

Vision Resources
Ponsonby, Auckland, New Zealand

Lifestream
Nottingham, England

WA Buchanan Company
Geebung, Queensland, Australia

Rhema Ministries Trading
Randburg, South Africa

Word Alive
Niverville, Manitoba, Canada

Salvation Book Centre
Petaling, Jaya, Malaysia

Vine Christian Centre
Mid Glamorgan, Wales, United Kingdom

Successful Christian Living
Capetown, Rep. of South Africa

Inside the U.S., call toll free to order:
1-800-722-6774

Dedication

To my father, the Reverend G.J. Bersche, who was also my spiritual father, who prepared me for life and ministry.

To my sons, Timothy and Kevin, whose pursuits of God and resultant godly lives cause my heart to rejoice and make me confident; my grandchildren, Benjamin, Jill, Jeremiah, and Luke, will learn the ways of God from their fathers.

To the many spiritual sons and daughters in whom my wife Carolyn and I have had the wonderful privilege of investing our lives. Especially to Nancy Webb and Todd Mielke, our first committed spiritual children who were serious about being prepared to walk with God and lead His Church.

To these persons, with whom I learned the principles expressed in these chapters, I dedicate this book.

Acknowledgments

All my love and much thanks to Carolyn, my wife of 39 years, who is a constant encouragement to me. She has been my personal prayer warrior all these years, and she challenges me to keep "pressing on" into Jesus! Thanks Carolyn.

Much thanks to Chris Thomas for the hundreds of hours she spent transcribing taped messages so the editing process could begin. What a blessing you are!

To Maureen, my faithful secretary of many years, who handles all the extra details that give that final touch to what I do. I am so thankful for your commitment!

To these and many others who challenge me to "excel still more" I give my thanks and love.

Endorsements for *Is There a Father in the House?*

"*Is There a Father in the House?* gives insight into both the why and the how to nurture and develop our young people into strong leaders. This timely book will bring change all across urban America. Thank you, Paul, for giving us the kind of understanding we need to be faithful 'fathers in the house.'"

>Eddie Edwards
>President and Founder
>Joy of Jesus Ministries
>Detroit, Michigan

"Throughout the nation a cry continues to rise from the hearts of the sons and daughters of our culture, a cry for fathers. ...I believe...*Is There a Father in the House?* illustrates and further clarifies the need and the 'how to's' of 'fathering' in the natural and in the church family."

> Don Crossland
> President and Founder
> Journey Toward Wholeness Ministries
> Little Rock, Arkansas

"...my friend Paul Bersche calls leaders to true spiritual fatherhood and thus satisfies the eternal mandate to create man in the image of God."

> Francis Frangipane
> Senior Pastor, River of Life Ministries
> Cedar Rapids, Iowa

"Communicating in his real-life-application style, ...Paul has captured the vital biblical principle of spiritual fathering. I am excited that someone has practically addressed the challenge of developing our 'fatherless' young people into mature Christian leaders."

> Michael A. Rosemond
> Michigan State Director
> Promise Keepers

"The absence of 'true fathers' has created serious ramifications to both the family and the Church. This book takes an engaging and provocative look at the need for spiritual fathers from a biblical perspective. My friend, Paul Bersche, truly exemplifies the essence of his message."

>Ellis L. Smith
>Senior Pastor
>Jubilee Christian Church
>Detroit, Michigan
>Co-host with Paul Bersche of dynamic
>   television program
>*The Good News in Black and White*

"In a day when children are becoming fathers, and fathers are forsaking children, this clarifying word comes from a man who is known among us as a 'father to many' in the Kingdom of God. As both exhorter and example, 'Pastor Paul' gives much-needed definition to the seasons of sonship and fatherhood, with principles that can be applied across the lines of natural and spiritual parenting. This book is excellent for both established and developing leaders, as well as parents and children."

>Rev. Sylvia R. Evans
>Executive Director, Women's Division
>Elim Fellowship
>Lima, New York
>Director/Founder, Creative Word Ministries
>Waycross, Georgia

Contents

Preface xiii
Foreword xv
Introduction xvii

Part 1   **The Cry for Spiritual Fathers** 1
     Chapter 1   Spiritual Anarchy 3
     Chapter 2   Four Mighty Weapons 15
     Chapter 3   The Days of Our Life 25
     Chapter 4   Sowing and Reaping 37

Part 2   **Raising Children** 47
     Chapter 5   God's Word and God's Man 49
     Chapter 6   Generations of Righteousness . . 55
     Chapter 7   Harnessing Maturity 61
     Chapter 8   Seasonal Transitions 71
     Chapter 9   Growing Up Fatherless 81

Part 3   **Equipping Young Men** 89
     Chapter 10   One Under Discipline 91
     Chapter 11   Five Keys to Fathering 105

Part 4	**Fathers and Mentors**	**121**
	Chapter 12 Moses and Joshua	123
	Chapter 13 Elijah and Elisha	133
	Chapter 14 Paul and Timothy	141
Part 5	**Unleashing Mature Sons**	**149**
	Chapter 15 Characteristics of a Mature Son	151
	Chapter 16 Unleashing Sons With Power	165

Preface

Jesus said the Father loves the Son and shows Him all things which He Himself is doing (Jn. 5:20). In the divine image we see the human model: Fathers loving sons and engaging in relationships that communicate not only knowledge but life. In this book, my friend Paul Bersche, calls leaders to true spiritual fatherhood and thus satisfies the eternal mandate to create man in the image of God.

>Frances Frangipane
>Senior Pastor
>River of Life Ministries
>President
>Advancing Church Ministries
>Cedar Rapids, Iowa

Foreword

Throughout the nation a cry continues to rise from the hearts of the sons and daughters of our culture, a cry for fathers. Multiple studies and statistics remind us of the correlation between our social problems and other issues that may be traced, directly or indirectly, to the failure of fathers to fulfill their vital and God-given responsibilities. Most fathers are missing the necessary skills to actually "father" their sons and daughters. Their abandonment of responsibility is not usually a planned attempt to fail, but it is due to a lack of training, modeling, empowerment, and motivation.

When I first met Paul and Carolyn Bersche several years ago, I was deeply impacted by their family life and its result in the lives of their two adult sons. It was obvious the hand of God was on their family.

I would have probably continued to respect their family life without asking any additional questions; however, I kept meeting others from outside of their natural family, young men and women whose lives have been deeply affected and touched by their influence. This included various ministers who they have helped to restore to ministry. My interest and desire to learn led me to ask specific questions to these various persons, questions like, "What characteristic in Paul's life do you most admire?" and "What have Paul and Carolyn done to help you the most?" The answers were consistent, "They are Christlike in their integrity, compassion, discipline, and their relationships. They are role models who live what they teach."

I believe that Paul Bersche's book *Is There a Father in the House?* illustrates and further clarifies the need and the "how to's" of "fathering" in the natural and in the church family. I pray this book will help the Body of Christ to take another significant step closer to "turning the hearts of the fathers to their children" (see Lk. 1:17).

>Don Crossland
>President and founder
>Journey Toward Wholeness Ministries
>Author of *A Journey Toward Wholeness*,
>>which describes how the healing power of
>>Christ's authority over sin and guilt
>>may be discovered.

Introduction

The news had captivated my heart. Over a period of several weeks it seemed the media was filled with stories about fatherless kids. I watched, listened to, and read story after story of this present reality of kids without fathers—fathers physically or psychologically absent from a place of positive influence in the lives of their children. Deep in my innermost being I kept hearing, "This is a fatherless generation."

During these weeks I meditated and prayed a great deal about what it was that the Father was saying to my spirit. Though I am aware that this book is far from an exhaustive study of the subject of spiritual fathers, it is nonetheless the Father's message and ministry to me for this time. I also believe the Lord revealed to me some important things concerning this fatherless generation and His desire for fathering sons and daughters. It seemed I couldn't shake it. I heard it over and over again: "This is a fatherless generation."

The Natural Explains the Spiritual

The apostle Paul said, "...the spiritual is not first, but the natural; then the spiritual" (1 Cor. 15:46). As I recalled these words it became very clear to me that what is happening in the natural is really an illustration of what is happening in the spiritual realm and in the Church! There are so many young men and women in our churches whose fathers have either physically abandoned them through divorce or spiritually abandoned them through disobedience. No wonder the truth of God's Word seems to bounce off their hearts and fails to effect change in their lives. There are not many "fathers" who will, teach the Word diligently to their children and talk of it with them in the house and as they walk by the way (see Deut. 6:7), teaching them to apply truth to everyday living.

What Happened to the Fathers?

During this time I was reading the Book of Judges. These words went deep into my spirit: "And all that generation also were gathered to their fathers; and there arose another generation after them *who did not know the Lord, nor yet the work which He had done* for Israel" (Judg. 2:10).

I cried! What happened to the fathers? Didn't they pass on in word and life the heritage of righteousness and spiritual leadership to their world? Why didn't these sons know God? A Jewish friend of mine who ministers with "Jews for Jesus" once told me that the reason orthodox

Jews are so intense about training their children in orthodoxy is because they live with the concern that they are only one generation away from forgetting God.

In the United States, we now have the first generation in the history of our nation that has no spiritual foundation. The children of the "baby boomers" (the "Boomers" born between 1946 and 1964) are recognized by at least two terms, "Generation X" or the "Baby Busters" (the "Busters" were born between 1964 and 1983). They are devoid of spiritual roots. This new generation of Americans is as heathen in their ways of thinking as those people in other nations to whom we used to send missionaries.

The Elisha Generation

This is why young men and women in the Church of Jesus today *must* have spiritual fathers and mothers. This generation must be prepared to bear the powerful double-portion anointing of God intended to lead His Church to its destiny and final glory. Spiritually mature saints must be encouraged to accept the challenge of drawing to themselves many sons and daughters. We must call forth and prepare our own children as well as those "spiritually orphaned" young people who seem to have been neglected in the church. It is a privilege for older saints to be involved in forming maturity in the lives of younger saints by teaching them "a more excellent way." Maturity is achieved when a young man or woman has learned to be submissive, obedient, responsible, and accountable.

Imagine the potential power of the Church in the next generation. Young men and women will be filled with the powerful double-portion anointing of God. They will be established in the Word and strengthened by maturity. That is what the church of spiritual fathering will prepare. *"Is There a Father in the House?"*

Part 1

The Cry for Spiritual Fathers

As for the days of our life, they contain seventy years, or if due to strength, eighty years, yet their pride is but labor and sorrow; for soon it is gone and we fly away. Who understands the power of Thine anger, and Thy fury, according to the fear that is due Thee? So teach us to number our days, that we may present to Thee a heart of wisdom.
Psalm 90:10-12

Chapter 1

Spiritual Anarchy

The way human beings relate to one another can often have an impact on God's ability to reach a generation. A time from the history of the nation of Israel clearly demonstrates this fact. The great leaders, Moses and Joshua, were dead. Without their guidance and control the people seemed lost. For over a hundred years God raised up one leader after another to deliver the people from their troubles. When God raised up a man to bring deliverance, the people were faithful and followed the Lord. When the leader died, the people fell back into their old sinful ways and habits.

Several generations of Israelites lived without clear leadership. They had the writings of Moses and the traditions of the feasts, sacrifices, and festivals, but they simply didn't follow the right path unless someone led them in the right direction. When they had no leader or judge, they did whatever they wanted. Judges 21:25 reads, "In those days there was no king in Israel; everyone did what was right in his own eyes." This period of history illustrates the depth of anarchy to which people will undoubtedly fall when they are unsubmissive, disobedient, unaccountable, and irresponsible. It also illustrates the need for the clear leadership of experienced spiritual fathers.

Anarchy in Christianity

In many respects the Church today appears to be in a state of anarchy. There are hundreds of denominations. Each presents a unique perspective or aspect of understanding. There are thousands of independent churches that are not affiliated with any of the established structures. A number of these denominations and groups have come about because someone wanted to do his or her own thing rather than follow established leadership. Certainly not all of this diversity is negative though; a centralized hierarchy of the Body of Christ has been definitely shown to be dangerous at best. However, the existence of so many groups shows us that many people have their hearts set on not following established leadership.

For centuries, people learned what it took to survive and thrive in society from their parents, tribal leaders, or a tradesman. Information was passed along from one generation to the next through apprenticeships and established family enterprises. Often sons would simply follow their fathers in the family business. Their work in that trade or business usually began in early childhood. The education or information needed to thrive was passed from father to son and from tradesman to apprentice.

This form of education and socialization instilled into young people a great deal of respect for the previous generation. A son would accept the views and training of his father. However, great change struck the trade and agricultural societies of the mid-eighteenth century when small machines were developed. New materials were created and developed. New sources of power were discovered and harnessed. Cities grew as people moved away from their rural communities and small towns. Even now in the Information Age, the industrial revolution continues relentlessly on with the constant development of new technology and electronic media.

I believe the industrial revolution contributed to the destruction of society and to the destruction of much authority in the Church of Jesus. Until the industrial revolution, we understood that each generation prepared the generation that followed it. The younger generation depended on the older generation to provide their preparation for life.

A son was trained by his father to take over whatever type of business the family practiced, whether it was a bakery, shoe shop, or dress shop. Through the father's training the son was prepared for his future, financially, morally, and spiritually. One of the effects of the industrial revolution was that a resistant attitude became planted in the hearts of many sons. It caused them to think. *I don't need to do what Dad did. I'm smarter than Dad. My dad was so old-fashioned he couldn't think beyond staying on the farm all those years and living a quiet and unchallenging life.*

Sons rejected the lives of their fathers; they felt they were dull. Perhaps the life style their parents represented was too much like that of the prodigal son's father, and it wasn't full enough of the world for them. The industrial revolution released young people to get jobs on their own, make their own money, and do their own thing. "Every man did that which was right in his own eyes" (See Judg. 21:25).

Now, the industrial revolution wasn't all wrong. It encouraged higher education, creativity, and ingenuity. But for the most part the attitudes that were born in the hearts of men during this period had a a destructive influence on society and the Church.

Independence vs. Interdependence

What kept the Church alive at the beginning of the industrial revolution was that it did not conform to the world's ways. The spirit of interdependence continued in the Church for many years in the face of the growing spirit of independence in the world. Interdependence gave the Church strength and stability. Christians knew they needed one another. This caused interdependence to die harder in the Church than in the world. Yet the independent spirit, which was so prevalent in the world, began to creep slowly into the Church. For the first few years of the industrial revolution, the Church of Jesus maintained its strength through continuing on with its interdependent spirit, but it finally succumbed to the overwhelming independent spirit of the world. However, the seeds of that interdependent spirit that had been planted in the Church in earlier years were preserved. They began to reap that same spirit of interdependence again among a remnant. Even today there are some older and wiser men and women who still carry that seed and continue to plant it once again in the Church.

The industrial revolution created independent-minded people who grew up thinking and living only for themselves, a direct contradiction to the Scripture's challenge to look out for one another (see Phil. 2:4). It seems we have adopted the world's view and attitudes as we in the Church of Jesus now model the old saying, "after me, you come first." Even when we gather to worship and fellowship together we have "me first" blinders on. We don't see the lady sitting next to us with tears in her eyes. We don't see the man with a sad face sitting in the pew across the way. We fail to see the desperation of the young person on our street or in the mall whose behavior we consider "unbecoming." We overlook the older persons whose loneliness should be instantly obvious from their facial expressions and body language. We don't see them because our own needs keep us crying out, "Won't somebody please notice me and help me?"

Each one of us needs to understand that if we don't notice them, they won't notice us. So we stand around in our churches looking forlorn, hoping someone will notice us, talk with us, and help us. We must learn that in the order of God we receive loving, caring ministry in the measure that we are willing to give it.

Psalm 90:12a says, "So teach us to number our days." Why? Because we only have 70 years on this earth to accomplish God's callings and purposes for our lives in His Kingdom, which may be extended to 80 by reason of strength given to us by God (see Ps. 90:10). That means we only have 70 to 80 years to provide for the generations in our care and prepare them to experience all that God wants to do in our world and His Kingdom through their lives. I've reached the stage in my own life where I've become fully aware that God is raising up a generation of young men and women who will take the forefront of leadership in the coming promised move of God in the Church. We older folks will probably live to see it happen, but we won't be leading it; we will have fathered sons and daughters to lead it. But we will still be in the background giving loving encouragement, and we'll be delighting in the powerful double-portion anointing on our spiritual offspring.

The same independent spirit that first expressed itself during the early days of the industrial revolution continues today. When young men and women rise into leadership, they often forget the wisdom of the previous generation. Young men may receive training and wisdom from elders and fathers of the Church, yet when they rise to leadership, zeal overwhelms clear memory. Soon the wisdom, impact, influence, authority, and anointing of their fathers are forgotten. Historically, this has been exemplified in every new move of God; the leaders of the new move persecute the leaders of the previous one. All too often the young people who have risen up to give leadership to the new movement speak unwisely, disrespectfully, and unrighteously of the leadership of the previous move of God. In the process they forget that those are the very folks who gave them their place of leadership and preparation for this new move of God. Then history continues to repeat itself in the next generation.

Thankfully, my natural and spiritual father, the Reverend G.J. Bersche, taught me very early in my ministry to honor those elders and fathers who have prepared the way of God before us. Their sacrifices and commitment to God should be remembered because their openness to God's Holy Spirit set the stage for my generation to experience and lead a three-year revival. My dad taught me to revere those old leaders of our denomination because their knowledge of God and His ways formed the foundation for my own recognition of the power of interdependence in the

Kingdom of God. Simply said, it was because of the elders and fathers who went before us that we were prepared to hear and receive from God in the "new move" of revival we have experienced.

Independence means to stand alone. It is a prideful attitude that claims, "I do not need anyone else to accomplish God's will in life." However, interdependence is a godly concept; we all need to depend on one another. We must trust one another. We *need* others in order to do what God wants us to do. Currently God is breaking down that resistant, prideful attitude in the Church, for that attitude of the world has no place in the Body of Christ. Often we wonder why God is not moving as we would like to see Him move. I believe this is because His timing will parallel the timing of the Church as it returns to interdependence. His heart's desire is for an interdependent, unified Church.

A Challenge During Captivity

Simply stated, *interdependence* is "I need you and you need me." As Christians, we no longer have a choice about loving one another. Jesus commanded, "Love one another" (see Jn. 15:12). In life you can pick your friends, but you're stuck with your relatives. In the Body of Christ we are all relatives. The prophet Jeremiah gave a challenge 2,600 years ago that still resounds true to the Church today:

> *Build houses and live in them; and plant gardens, and eat their produce. Take wives and become the fathers of sons and daughters, and take wives for your sons and give your daughters to husbands, that they may bear sons and daughters; and multiply there and do not decrease.*
>
> Jeremiah 29:5-6

The Church today is in much the same position as was experienced by the children of Israel in Jeremiah's time. During this time the Israelites were in captivity to pagans. Today, the Church has become captive to pagan ideas from the world, particularly the pagan idea of independence. God told the Israelites that while they were in captivity (and I believe, prophetically, we are still in captivity) they would build the Kingdom of God. Obey the command to have sons and daughters. Then teach your sons to have sons and daughters. Make sure that your sons get the right wives, and make sure that your daughters get the right husbands. Continue to build the Kingdom.

I believe Jeremiah's message to the Israelites is also Jesus' word for us today. We must take responsibility for the next generation of believers. All you have to do is start where you are, regardless of your current season of life. Start being in obedience to God wherever you are. What you plant in this season, you will reap in the next one. Don't frustrate the grace of God. God's instruction is to raise up men of understanding—naturally and spiritually. He is showing us the necessity of bringing forth sons. Even in the midst of the captivity, where it seems like the wicked one has absolute control, we cannot say we ought not bring forth sons.

Natural Fear and Spiritual Weakness

The natural explains the spiritual. People are saying today, "What an awful day to have children. I would be very frightened to have children today." The response to that is, absolutely not! I know that I may sound like a radical, but it is as though we are captive in Babylon and have the opportunity to teach our children to raise up more children. Now when the Church is freed from Babylon (the world), we will overflow the land with righteous seed. Bring forth sons and daughters. Teach them to bring forth sons and daughters. Raise up men to live in the righteousness of God. Teach them to strengthen the foundation of the Kingdom of God.

When God spoke that word through Jeremiah, the older men began to sing the songs of Zion again. When they sang the songs of Zion, the hearts of the people were warmed, and they began to move toward God once again. As they were released from Babylon they went back to Jerusalem and rebuilt the righteous city. They went back in three waves. When the third wave of God's people came to Jerusalem, the wave was so strong that the unrighteousness there couldn't stand against it. That's why your role is so powerful in the Kingdom of God whether you are a spiritual son or a spiritual father. You are part of the last wave of saints who will bring in the final glory of the Church in these last days.

Spiritual anarchy has crept into the Church. The pervasive attitude of our day seems to be one of independence. Everyone is doing whatever they want. But God is calling us to be a people who are free from captivity even in the midst of captivity. He is calling us to look to the future and bring forth sons. This generation can and will release a generation into the world that will shake the world with the power of God, and it will happen as God's people see the need to invest in sons and daughters. Then nothing can stop the unified, interdependent Church of Jesus Christ.

Chapter 2

Four Mighty Weapons

I have a new understanding in my spirit regarding why God sent the wicked one to this earth rather than locking him up in hell. When we truly capture this down in our spirits, I believe it will transform us. We will finally become the confident faith-filled believers we long to be.

Consider this: when a judge in a court of law sends a man to prison, he sends him to prison to be bound and punished. Prison becomes a place of torment to him. Well, when God sent satan to this earth he wasn't saying, "There, go play and wreck havoc until I come back again. Just go ahead and destroy all the people you desire. When you are finished wrecking everything, I'll come back and rescue My suffering people from your destructive schemes." No, God sent satan to this earth as a judge sends a man who has committed a crime to prison.

God sent satan to earth to be tormented. Who torments him here? He's tormented by you and me—God's people! How do we torment him? By the praises of our lips and the righteousness of our lives. As we walk in righteousness, it torments the wicked one. As we walk in obedience to the Word of God, repent of our sins, and express our praise to God in all things, the wicked one is frustrated in his plans for our lives, he begins to think it might have been better for him to have been locked up in hell.

Understanding this principle causes all of the little things that upset and frustrate us to simply lose their impact. Ephesians 3:10 reads, "in order that the manifold wisdom of God might now be made known *through the Church* to the rulers and the authorities in the heavenly places." Notice that it is *through the Church* that He brings the authority, the knowledge, and the wisdom of God against the powers of darkness. It is through you and me! We have been given the delight of causing the wicked one great misery during his stay on the earth.

In my view, the wicked one has only two weapons in his arsenal to use against us, deception and accusation. He tries to overcome God's people by encouraging them to accuse one another. He even has the boldness to try to accuse us before God and the angels. By deceiving the people of God, he limits our discernment, faith, and power. He works to stop the praise of righteous lips from tormenting him.

Allow me to illustrate the effectiveness of his deception upon us. Satan loves there to be undefined silence between believers. This is usually born out of misunderstanding, misinterpretation, or misinformation, but oh how he loves this scenario. The folks on the various sides of an issue wait impatiently in this undefined silence. Very quickly satan will come to interpret the silence for us. He assures us that we are right, at least "more right" than the others and that "they" surely have need of repentance and restoration, not us. These deceptions bring the accusations that tumble around in our minds and create great distress over something that would have been easily resolved simply by going to the brother and letting him interpret his own silence (see Mt. 18:15). Remember, our resources to overcome satan are "mighty through God to the pulling down of strongholds" (see 2 Cor. 10:4 KJV).

The Right Intercession

Intercession is a powerful weapon in overcoming our enemy satan. But I also believe prayer intercession without the foundational backdrop of living intercession is ineffective in the spirit realm. Let me explain: I believe we need to be powerful in our intercession, but I'll tell you I'm weary of the kind of intercession that simply stomps, screams, groans, fakes tears, and speaks in tongues with angry faces and fists doubled up in fighting readiness. All of this is intended to frighten the devil off and bind him from further effectiveness against God's people and purposes. I don't think he is frightened at all by any of it.

All of the screaming, shouting, hard praying, prophesying will never accomplish anything of itself. No wonder the wicked one doesn't leave us alone after all that. He's not moved by an intercessor's words or forcefulness; rather, he's moved by the intercessor's life of obedience. The fact that the intercessor's life is a living demonstration of the righteousness of God causes the words he prays to have authority and anointing.

Without that life of authority and anointing our words will do nothing to stop the wicked one. Satan does not fear our words unless our lives are a living demonstration of those words. To bring down a stronghold of satan, our lives must express the living truth of God in opposition to that stronghold. Then our active intercessory prayers will have the power to defeat the enemy of our souls.

Edwin Cole, a respected teacher of men, says "the man is more than the message" and "Christ-likeness and manhood are synonymous." You can *talk* all you want but the *life* of the man is what is important. A life style of righteousness, offering up acceptable sacrifices to God is what challenges the enemy. Prayer is not using magic words to bring down satan. Prayer is the cry of a righteous heart that pierces the enemy through and through. Intercessory prayer is not so much for bringing down strongholds and chasing off the devil as it is for bringing in the glory of God—from which the devil flees and by which strongholds fall.

HERO: Weapons of the Kingdom

In addition to becoming living and praying intercessors, we have four mighty weapons given to us by God to keep satan from breaking through and frustrating the grace of God in our lives. These four weapons are character traits, which are worked into the fabric of our lives by the Spirit of God. I want to introduce them to you by using the acronym "HERO."

> H—humility
> E—endurance
> R—repentance
> O—obedience

Let's look briefly at each one.

Humility

Please understand that the Word of God says "humble yourselves, therefore, under the mighty hand of God..."

(1 Peter 5:6). Don't ask God to humble you; He has given that responsibility to us. He says you are to humble yourself under the mighty hand of God. How is that done? Humility is simply me agreeing with God that He knows all about me. I agree with His assessment that I am merely a man who desperately needs Him every moment of my life. Every accomplishment and every fulfillment in my life is His wonderful grace at work in me for His purposes. Humility involves a joining with God's sane estimate of who He has made and gifted me to be in His Kingdom. What a weapon against satan! All of satan's temptations designed to move us outside the purposes of God have no effect on a humble heart.

Endurance

The Scriptures tell us that "the one who endures to the end will be saved" (Mt. 24:13). However, we also need to apply endurance to the here and now. If we quit every project before we have done all we can do, we do not understand endurance. If we give up on others without giving God the time to work or without giving them the opportunity to change, we are not practicing endurance. In John 21:3-6 the disciples had fished all night without catching anything. Jesus told them to cast their net again on the other side of the boat. They were tired, and they wanted to go home. Yet they endured. They cast out the net one last time. That catch was bigger than their boat could hold. An enduring heart makes it very difficult for satan to break us down through disappointment and multiplied frustrations.

Repentance

Repentance is not an event. Repentance is a life style. I am weary of God's people spending only two weeks out of the year in repentance (spring and fall "revival" at church) while the rest of the year is devoted to a life of compromise. The conviction becomes so great we cannot stand it any longer, so twice a year we repent and get "revived." This is not God's way. He speaks of repentance as a way of life for His people. Repentance makes us willing to have a change of mind. We recognize that living our own way is rebellion against God. Repentance is sorrow for bringing pain to God's heart by not living His way. Repentance means living a life of love and commitment to God. Human beings fail, but an attitude and life style of repentance brings growth from our failures and restores us to the Christ-likeness God intends. Satan cannot stand against a repentant heart. It torments him to find a person so desirous of pleasing God because his temptations to please self have little or no effect on a repentant heart.

Obedience

I'd like you to notice that as you write the word *obedience* the middle letters spell *die*, d-i-e to your own ways. Like the apostle Paul we must "die daily" (see 1 Cor. 15:31). When our will is in submission to His Word and will, the wicked one's temptations are tested against the truth of the Word of God, and our choice will be to obey Him—no matter the cost. Watch your children when you tell them to do something they don't want to do. Often they will react as if it was killing them to obey you. God desires choices of obedience that flow out of our loving commitment to Him. He desires us to make our choices with glad hearts. Satan cannot break down the heart that has an undivided, loving commitment to God. He knows that heart will choose to obey God, so he remains tormented and frustrated in his efforts to conquer our lives.

A Victorious Church Generation

What does all this have to do with spiritual fathers and sons?

We have a very real enemy who would like nothing more than to destroy this Church generation. Over the centuries he has tried to destroy the Church many times. However, God's Church has always stood its ground. In every generation spiritual fathers have risen to mentor others in how to live, move, and have their being in Jesus Christ (see Acts 17:28). They have modeled and taught the "HERO" character traits. Today's Church has become clouded by the world, but God is raising a generation who will stand in victory over the enemy.

This generation has made great strides in restoring New Testament principles and truths to the Church. We have come a long way. The next generation can be a generation of God's Church that will not forget Him. It can be a heroic generation that will use its strength of character to defeat the enemy at every hand. The next generation can be a Church that will obey God rather than man. For this to happen and for the next generation to experience a double portion of the anointing, *this* generation will have to allow God to raise us up as spiritual fathers. The next generation, the Kingdom, and the future will each be impacted in proportion to our willingness to serve the needs of those who come after us.

Chapter 3

The Days of Our Life

The "Times and Seasons" in the Process of Preparing Spiritual Fathers

Warning—Don't blow this season also!
Endure and Overcome!
Sowing/Reaping Principle (Galatians 6:7-10)!

Four Jurisdictions: (2 Cor. 10:12-18) —measure —sphere (Influence)	Individual (Conscience)	Household (Generosity) Economics Education	The Church (Truth) Illumine truth to everyday life!	God's Kingdom and Man's Government (Justice) Righteousness
		Our Influence and Impact in Each Season		
		Spiritual and Moral Influence		
Four Seasons and Four Adventures of Life	Preparation: Study Hospitality Business	Production: Babies and Business Hospitality Study (Elder/Father)	Provision: Hospitality Business Spiritual Father Study	Protection: Spiritual Father Hospitality Business Study
Spiritual Realm Progression of Growth (1 Jn. 2:12-14)	Child "…because your sins are forgiven for His name's sake." "…because you know His Father."	Young Man "…because you have overcome the evil one…." "…because you are strong and the Word of God abides in you…."	Father (Elder) "…because you know Him who has been from the beginning."	Spiritual Father "…for in Christ Jesus I became your father through the gospel." (1 Cor. 4:15b)
Natural Realm Progression of Growth	Child—Teen Submission Obedience Responsibility Accountability (Unto Maturity)	Parent Responsibility Accountability	Grandparent Posterity Heritage	Great Grandparent Patriarch Matriarch
20-Year Age Segments of Our Lives	0	20	40	60 80

Initial inspiration from Greg Harris' chart from
"The Seasons of Life Seminar."

Christian Life Workshops
180 S. E. Kane Road
Gresham, OR 97080

The natural process of human development points to a great spiritual truth. As we develop, grow, and mature as human beings, we go through many different stages, seasons, and levels of growth. Every one of the seasons is important in the process of becoming fully aware of and able to reach our potential. We start out as infants, totally dependent on our parents. Later, we develop skills that enable us to relate to others and grow in maturity. Human life involves going through periods of training and preparation, production and fruitfulness, wisdom, and contribution to others. The final level, being a spiritual father, is the stage when we can make the greatest impact on the world and the Kingdom of God.

When I speak of fathering, I am not speaking exclusively of fatherhood. According to the Word of God, there is also a mothering of daughters in the Kingdom. The same principles of God work in the lives of men and women. God's children are not limited by gender. Women and men can both apply these principles of spiritual fathering to achieve the greatest possible impact.

The Secret of Endurance

We addressed the issue of endurance briefly in the last chapter. However, as we look at the different seasons of life a more complete examination of this important principle will be helpful. Psalm 90:10 reads, "As for the days of our life, they contain seventy years, or if due to strength, eighty years, yet their pride is but labor and sorrow; for soon it is gone and we fly away." I want you to clearly understand something. When we begin to understand that the way of God has sorrow and affliction in it, we begin to live with realistic spiritual expectations. We become enabled by God to be an overcomer in the midst of sorrow and affliction.

One of the things God wants fathers to teach their sons is how to endure. We must learn how to endure hardness as a good soldier (2 Tim. 2:3). We need to endure all the way through. In God's understanding, enduring doesn't mean just gritting your teeth and holding on until it's over. Enduring means recognizing that this hardship is ordered of God. Like Paul, we must embrace this grace work of God and say, "Thank you, Lord. I understand God is at work in me to will and to do His good pleasure. So, Lord, since this is You at work, I will endure hardness as a good soldier. I will hold fast to You during this time knowing that when it is over you will have worked your good work in me. Therefore, I yield to You now, and I will not try to avoid this time in my life. I will walk in obedience to You regardless of the pressures exerted against me. Thank You for loving me so much." (See Philippians 2:13; Second Timothy 2:3.)

Enduring brings on the blessing of God. He who endures to the end will be saved (see Mt. 24:13). Now understand God is not talking about being born again. He is talking about the process of salvation. Salvation is not simply a one-time thing. The Scriptures indicate three different aspects of our salvation. We are *saved*, in other words, born again; we are *being saved*, which is the process of our growing up in God; and we *shall be saved* when Jesus comes to receive us unto Himself. When you are born again, you are in the process of salvation. The process of salvation becomes completed as we endure to the end.

James, the brother of Jesus, wrote "Blessed is a man who perseveres under trial; for once he has been approved, he will receive the crown of life, which the Lord has promised to those who love Him (Jas. 1:12). So endure. We need to destroy the myth that says, "Now that you are born again, everything will be just the way you like it." The wicked one uses this lie against young saints in particular. We like to think that things will go our way because we have been born again. Eventually we find out that our way isn't God's way. God's way has some hardness, difficulty, and frustration in it. We may be in shock, but we still need to endure. Through endurance we begin to understand the workings of God.

Numbering Our Days

Psalm 90:11-12 explains, "Who understands the power of Thine anger, and Thy fury, according to the fear that is due Thee? So teach us to number our days, that we may present to Thee a heart of wisdom." We must endure so that when we come before the Lord we may present to Him a heart of wisdom. We are not going to fade out on God. We are going to make a presentation to Him. We will learn wisdom through what we experience so we may present our heart of wisdom to Him.

What is a heart of wisdom? Solomon spoke of knowledge, understanding, and wisdom. *Knowledge* is knowing about life from God's perspective. *Understanding* is seeing life from God's perspective, and *wisdom* is living life from God's perspective and giving it away to others. So the "heart of wisdom" that we present to God is our life lived from God's perspective and shared with others so they too may present "a heart of wisdom" to God as well! This is the ministry of spiritual fathers; they give away the wisdom God has vested in them preparing the next generation to be godly and wise men and women.

Preparation

As we have already noticed in Psalm 90:10 we have approximately 80 years to live in this world. I see it like this: our 80 years are divided into four seasons of 20 years each. The first 20 years are for preparation. These are the years of our growing up, training in personhood, character building, and receiving the education that leads to adulthood. I love having young people in my life. They have learner's hearts. It is a wonderful opportunity to be able to direct their passion for God and for His purposes. Yet they can also be so undisciplined, irresponsible, and unsubmissive that the wisdom of God in you will be challenged to the limit.

Often young people receive a dream or vision from God or someone prophesies over them, and they think they are ready to see the vision fulfilled immediately. Many times young people have said to me, "I have this word from God"; "I found this promise in the Word"; or "Somebody prophesied over me and there's been confirmation. I'm supposed to do this and that. I even had a dream about it last week, so what's the hold up? Why isn't it happening? I'm supposed to be speaking to thousands. Why I even saw a picture when the prophet spoke over me. He saw the same picture. So I know that's what I'm supposed to be doing. That's my purpose in life, my destiny. I have had it in my heart now for two months and it still isn't happening. *What is the delay?"*

We often fail to understand that God's plan is to reveal the future so we will do a better job of preparing for it. We must be prepared to carry the responsibility of the future He has planned for us. My usual response to an anxious young person is that he should be glad he doesn't live in the day of Moses. His seasons of life were much longer. Each of Moses' seasons lasted 40 years. Jesus waited until he was 30 before he started ministry. What's the hurry?

This first stage lasts about 20 years, although there can be a great deal of flexibility depending upon the person. It is a season of preparation. This is the time of training and schooling to get us ready for the next season of life. Please understand that what we sow, we reap. What we sow in preparation during our first 20 years, we will reap in the next 20 years of production. What we sow in this season will either heighten or limit the production of our lives in the following season.

Production

The next 20-year season is usually one of production, whether it is business or babies. There may be different variables and requirements during this period of life, but generally speaking the focus of this 20-year time frame is becoming established in a career and raising a family. This is not to say that in this season we are exclusively involved in career and family or other meaningful areas of life are unavailable, such as the ministry of your gifts and talents in the church. However, just as the focus of those first 20 years was preparation, the focus of the second 20 years is production. This is when you form the foundations for your family, career, or your business, and you find your place in the Body of Jesus Christ. It is a time of sensing and confirming your sense of calling.

Provision

The third season is a time of provision. This is the general focus of life for the person between 40 and 60 years old. By this time our babies and business responsibilities are stabilized. We are able to give more of ourselves to being a significant influence in the Body of Christ. These are more mature years. We have experienced a great deal that can be shared with those in the preparation and production years. We have the opportunity to cause those in the prior seasons to experience in their lives multiplied impact and influence in comparison to our own.

Please don't misunderstand, it isn't that we don't effectively give ourselves in the church during the first 40 years of life. We do, but now our experience, expertise, and giftings give us a place of increased authority and anointing. In this season we are free to pour out our lives without experiencing the distractions of the past seasons.

These are the years we can give ourselves to equipping and building up the Body of Christ with all we have learned from the Spirit of God by experience and revelation in raising our families and establishing our lives in Him, His Word, and His Ways. From the perspective of available time, we have a great deal more freedom to devote ourselves to the Body. The wealth of the riches of His grace that have been stored up within you can now be released into the Kingdom of God in greater measure.

Protection

The final phase is protection. This season comes when a person is 60 to 80 years old. By this time we have been well prepared. We have produced, and we have been given the provision of our lives to the life of the Body of Christ. Now our role, in our family, the Church, and in society at large, is to be a person of protection over all that God has put under our care. This is a time of Christian statesmanship. The Church is in need of statesmen. People who have developed a deep intimacy with God through their years of overcoming exert a powerful, holy influence on the life of the Church. Their lives of wisdom and first-hand knowledge and understanding of God and His ways give order and stability to the Church and its leaders as they lead the people of God to fulfill their destiny in Him.

There are folks who always want to say something, and there are those who have something to say. Those who have reached the years of eldership have a great deal to say. Their years of developed wisdom, as well as their understanding of the principles of Church order, make them a necessary voice in giving counsel and direction to the affairs of the Kingdom of God. The wisdom of your years of faithfulness is worth sharing, especially for the sake of the next generation.

Seasons of Life

In summary, the seasons of life, divided into approximately 20 years each, are preparation, production, provision, and protection. In the Body of Christ, we reap what we sow. If we sow an independent spirit in our own family or in the Church, there are those who watch us who will follow our example. I often say to the older folks in our congregation, especially to those in places of leadership, "You lead people whether you are aware of it or not. There are people who are noticing your life, your attitudes, your love for God, and your commitment to Him. They are receiving seed into their ground. Are they receiving a seed of independence and resistance or are they receiving the seed of humility, endurance, repentance, and obedience that builds an attitude of interdependence?" The role of the spiritual father is a powerful, mentoring role. Only God knows the degree of impact of those who will dare to be fathers in the Church of Jesus Christ.

Chapter 4

Sowing and Reaping

The issue of undisciplined children comes up over and over again in church settings. We often see children running in loose, unconstrained fashion in the home, in the church, and at the mall. Their parents seem oblivious to the fact that their children's undisciplined behavior negatively affects many people. I love to get young parents alone to challenge them. I explain to them that their two year old who is presently annoying will grow into a twelve year old who is dangerous, unless some proper order is planted in that child. Children must be *taught* to respect their elders and parents. It does not come naturally. Regardless of their words, children will follow the example of their parents. We will reap what we sow.

We have allowed young men and women in the Kingdom of God to hold a negative view of those who are older in the Lord. The unspoken attitude of their hearts is, "They had their day, but now they are old-fashioned and disconnected from the 'real world.' " These young people mentally relegated their elders to the pasture of spiritual uselessness. This is another result of the spiritual anarchy we looked at in Chapter 1. It is the grace of God that is allowing us to still progress toward the promised move of

God. It is not *because* of us it is *in spite of* us. We will still reap what we sow.

In a large measure it appears we have sown the seeds that are currently reaping a negative and destructive harvest. We have allowed our young people to fail to give honor and respect to those who are over them in the Lord. They have apparently followed the examples of their parents and leaders, and it is causing the Church to lose a wealth of experienced and wise counsel and the stabilizing strength it brings to the Church. It seems we have cultivated disrespect for elders, fathers, and statesmen, and the Church is now in desperate need of the wisdom and discernment these individuals can give. Yes, we do reap what we have sown.

The Jesus Movement

I recall a mighty revival a couple of decades ago known as the "Jesus Movement." The results of this wave of God can still be seen today. Many of the men leading ministries that are still strong, powerful, and growing, were in their younger years at the beginning of the Jesus movement. The impact and influence of these men is still increasing. They experience the blessing and the anointing of God on their ministry today because they gave honor to their elders as young men. They understood that the older men could give them wise counsel, for they had also walked in the great moves of God in their youth. The older saints had learned how to endure through hardness, physically, emotionally, and spiritually, and they had emerged "more than conquerors" (see Rom. 8:37). The men whose ministries are successful today were the leaders in the Jesus movement who gave honor to the leaders before them. These are the ones who now have great influence on the Church, the nation, and the world. Those leaders who had worked alongside these men but spoke unrighteously and unkindly about the previous move of God and its leadership are the men and women whose leadership has now faded. You no longer hear about them. We will reap what we sow.

The Spiritual Value of Maturity

Often as younger men start moving into leadership in the Church, their zeal causes them to ignore what has already happened because of the lives and leadership of the older men. They really need a renewed sense of history. They need to see how God used those men to prepare the way for their own leadership. I remind them to not forget who got them to this place—Jesus and His leaders of the past. Those older saints have been through the dealings of God, which made them spiritual heros—Humble, Enduring, Repentant, and Obedient! They have much wisdom and discernment to share that, effectively applied, will cause the present Church to experience mighty moves of God sooner and with more stability. Like the elders of the tribes of Israel, they have lived through the rise and fall and rising again of the Church. They know the way through the wilderness and they have been to Canaan. They can tell us what to avoid, what to join, and when to wait.

It is my privilege to be a spiritual father to some pastor friends. I delight in giving myself to these younger men. Recently as I sat across the table from a young pastor, my heart wanted to reach out to hold him and weep with him because of the story he was telling me about his family, his church, and the pain he was experiencing because of both. He felt there was no one he could trust to be his spiritual father. Someone had told him I would listen. He told me, "Somebody told me you cared about us, about pastors like me, so I took the chance and called you." Older saints have wisdom and discernment that will not only heal the pain but point the way through the wilderness.

In Due Time

> *Do not be deceived, God is not mocked; for whatever a man sows, this he will also reap. For the one who sows to his own flesh shall from the flesh reap corruption, but the one who sows to the Spirit shall from the Spirit reap eternal life. And let us not lose heart in doing good, for in due time we shall reap if we do not grow weary. So then, while we have opportunity, let us do good to all men, and especially to those who are of the household of faith.*
>
> Galatians 6:7-10

Don't lose heart in doing good. In due time we shall reap. I have come to the conclusion that time is not our enemy. Time is our friend. Time is God's way of making sure everything doesn't happen all at once. Isn't that good of God? He knows we could not handle it. Whatever is taking place at this season of your life, you need to be there to experience what you're experiencing. Before now, you couldn't have handled it. Keep in mind that God knows what He's doing.

In due time, God brought forth His Son born of a woman, not before time, in due time (see Gal. 4:4). Time is

God's way of making sure something does not happen before it is supposed to and to make sure something does happen when it is supposed to. Time is not our enemy. *We* are our enemy. God's whole purpose for the seasons of life is for us to learn to live a life of quiet. Paul instructed the Church to live a quiet life (see 1 Tim. 2:2). Simply said, a quiet life is a rested, unrushed, confident life because a person has learned that God truly is God, and that we have the privilege of being made into His image by His workings in us.

The seasons of life keep us from trying to make something happen in our lives prematurely. That's what disquiets our lives. We get up in the morning, and we want what we want to happen today. The day becomes the master of our schedule instead of God who made it to show His glory through our lives. That kind of day, stacked up upon many other days like it, will keep us from the quiet life. Our God has designed the seasons so we can rest in Him and know we are fulfilling His purposes for our destiny.

A child (from birth to age 20) must understand this is the period of preparation. He should delight in it, give himself to it. Never fight your season, rest in it.

The years of preparation are followed by the years of production. Not everybody will get married, have babies, open up a new business, or begin a new career in their early twenties. There is some flexibility with all of this, but this is primarily a season for babies and businesses. Your preparation time has now passed. You may still be doing some study and preparation, but that is not your focus. Nor is it yet your provision time; that's still ahead of you.

So rest in the season you are in. Don't go into a panic because you are not yet famous and haven't fulfilled your destiny. I keep telling some of our young men, "Remember Jesus. He didn't start until He was 30. Remember Moses, he didn't start until he was 80." Well that is not encouraging news to someone who is 26 years old.

The time of provision is God's time. Will you give yourself now, without distractions and hindrances, to the Body of Christ? You are past the time of babies and businesses. Now you are in the time for Kingdom building, the time to give the riches of the wisdom God has given you through the babies and business, through the experiences of humbling, enduring, and obeying. You have so much to give now. Many older folks have a negative response to involvement and ministry at this time. I often hear something like this, "I've given all I'm giving, I've served all I'm going to serve. It's time for me to sit back and let the young ones do it." Have you heard this message? The seasons God has established for our lives will lead us to more peace and less stress. Let us learn to yield to His work of making us into His image during these seasons of life. This is excellent preparation for becoming effective spiritual fathers.

A Call From the Future Harvest

Indeed, we reap what we sow. The seeds are to be seeds of blessing and peace rather than cursing and disquietness. Older saints who give up when they reach maturity fail to recognize they are at the point they can contribute the *most* to the Kingdom of God. Youth have more energy and zeal, but that energy must be tempered with wisdom. The wisdom God has vested in you as a spiritual father or mother will be that tempering balance in their lives. As you give these best years to the Kingdom of God, you will not shrivel or fade away. His life will flow through your wisdom and discernment.

A generation is calling. They are witnessing God's call from the future for a people to be spiritual parents so God's move can reach its complete potential. Plant some seeds in the field of God's young people and watch the bountiful harvest of revival that will grow from it in the next generation. The effort you make in bringing spiritual seed to maturity will impact eternity. We will reap what we sow.

Part 2

Raising Children

You, however, continue in the things you have learned and become convinced of, knowing from whom you have learned them; and that from childhood you have known the sacred writings which are able to give you the wisdom that leads to salvation through faith which is in Christ Jesus. All Scripture is inspired by God and profitable for teaching, for reproof, for correction, for training in righteousness; that the man of God may be adequate, equipped for every good work.

2 Timothy 3:14-17

Chapter 5

God's Word and God's Man

The hope of the next generation of believers depends on the solid foundation we establish today. The house God's building will be strong, mighty, and powerful in Him in direct correlation to how we are applying the truths of His Word and living as men and women of God. He is continually shaping us into His image. He wants to make us His people who will be able to use each of our seasons of life as building stones for the next generation. We have so much to contribute to His Kingdom, but it all boils down to God's Word and God's men living in obedience to that Word.

The Word

Notice what Peter wrote concerning the essential nature and quality of God's Word,

And so we have the prophetic word made more sure, to which you do well to pay attention as to a lamp shining in a dark place, until the day dawns and the morning star arises in your hearts. But know this first of all, that no prophecy of Scripture is a matter of one's own interpretation, for no prophecy was ever made by an act of human will, but men moved by the Holy Spirit spoke from God.
                                        2 Peter 1:19-21

The Scriptures confirm the importance of God's Word and God's man. As we've already seen, Edwin Cole teaches that Christlikeness and manhood are synonymous. There are examples throughout Scripture of God appointing His men to their place in Him. Were these men in their place because they were men of God's Word? God puts men into appointed places because they are men with the Word of God in them for that time and that place for those people.

God's Man

God does everything as a father. Look at Hebrews 3:1, "Therefore, holy brethren, partakers of the heavenly calling, consider Jesus the Apostle and High Priest of our confession." People often ask me, "How do you know what the Father God is like?" I think the answer is fairly easy. The Scriptures say "…Let Us make man in Our image…" (Gen. 1:26). Like father, like son: if you want to know what the Father is like, just look at the life of Jesus and you will see the Father.

We often say this in the natural, but remember, the natural explains the spiritual. We say "He looks like a chip off the old block." What God is doing is raising up spiritual fathers who will raise up spiritual sons who will look like them. This is the time for sons to be willing and for spiritual fathers to take responsibility.

> *He was faithful to Him who appointed Him, as Moses also was in all His house* [in all of God's house]. *For He has been counted worthy of more glory than Moses, by just so much as the builder of the house has more honor than the house. For every house is built by someone, but the builder of all*

> *things is God. Now Moses was faithful in all His house as a servant, for a testimony of those things which were to be spoken later; but Christ was faithful as a Son over His house whose house we are, if we hold fast our confidence and the boast of our hope firm until the end.*
>
> Hebrews 3:2-6

No matter how long we consider it, the word *all* means "all." Everything God does is done as a father. Fatherhood and the household of God go together. I believe that there is a concept in the Scriptures we need to capture. It is the concept of the "house"—the Church being the "house" of God. Every leader that God puts in place is a father of the house. Everything God does is as a father. The head of a particular group or ministry is the father of that household. You can't have a household without a father.

Our world would like to convince us that *household* has a new definition. Many claim that a household is just a group of people living together. But the principle of the Word of God can't be denied by God's people. It may be denied by the world, but God's people must not deny it. You can't have a household without a father. That is the order of God.

The Father's Will for Sons

A son does not pick the father, the father picks the son. I didn't choose to be born. My father chose for me to be born. It was my Father God who instigated the process of my birth. My parents came together by the initiation of the Holy Spirit, and I was conceived. My heavenly Father wanted a son who would walk with God. It was God's plan, not my father's or my mother's. I did not choose to be born. I was chosen.

It is the same in spiritual fathering. God brings sons into the spiritual fathers' lives. By His appointment the father chooses a son. You do not have to be an old man to be a spiritual father any more than you do to be a natural one. Mature young men may also be chosen by God for this ministry.

Society is built on natural and spiritual fathers. The Church is built on fathers chosen by God. Everything in the house depends on what the father does. The passage from Hebrews 3 shows us that Jesus was the Son in the house of the Father who was before Him. Jesus was the Son of the house, and now we are sons in His house. Everything in the house depends upon the father; the children of the house carry his genes.

Chapter 6

Generations of Righteousness

If you stay around churches long enough, you will observe honored pastoral leadership. You will see that each house carries the genes of the father of that house. If he is a man of worship, it will be a worshiping house. If he is a man of prayer, it will be a praying house. If he is a singing leader, then everybody in that house will sing. Those who follow him will pick up his style of teaching and speaking. They will use his phrasing and his favorite words because they are of his genes. It is only right that it should be that way. It is the way of God for the children carry their father's genes.

God is the father of the universe, Jesus is the father of His Church and the Kingdom of God. In the Church of Jesus, the set man, the head leader is the father of the house as God has chosen him. Let me share my heart on this whole matter.

From Generation to Generation

A man who rises to serve God not only blesses the present generation but he potentially sets in motion a blessing that will flow through generations to come. Remember, Moses said that unrighteousness, the sins of the fathers, is visited upon the children.

You shall not worship them or serve them; for I, the Lord your God, am a jealous God, visiting the iniquity of the fathers on the children, on the third and fourth generations of those who hate Me, but showing lovingkindness to thousands, to those who love Me and keep My commandments.

Exodus 20:5-6

The sins of the fathers are visited upon the children up to the fifth generation. This is evidence of the sowing and reaping principle discussed in Chapter 4. The righteousness of the fathers is visited upon the thousandth generation. So when you sow righteousness, you reap righteousness. Who can keep up with thousands of generations? That is the way our God is. He sets seasons, and He can see thousands of generations into the future from when He spoke a word. He can bring forth righteousness from that word that was planted in the hearts of fathers who also passed the word on to their children. Repentance of the sons will break the power of the sins of their fathers upon them.

Let me share a personal example. My grandfather on my father's side came over from Germany. He was a tough character. He was the owner of a saloon in Kentucky that resembled those of the early West (you know, complete with boardwalk and swinging doors). My dad told my brothers and me stories about that awful period of his childhood. The drunks in the bar would create a ring. Then they put my dad and his brothers in the ring and made them box and knock each other silly while the bar patrons bet on them.

My grandfather was an alcoholic. In his prime he was 6'3" or 6'4", weighed about 280 pounds. My grandmother was a little Irish woman who was 4'10". She weighed about 100 pounds. My grandfather would come home roaring drunk every night. My father told us stories of how his father beat my grandmother. She eventually died in a mental institution.

Dad first heard the gospel at the age of 16. He was born again and received the call to preach. My grandfather hated ministers and priests. He had taught his children to continue this hatred by saying, "If you see a priest or a minister walking on the street, get on the other side and spit on the ground. They're not worth the ground they walk on." Needless to say this created more than a little conflict when my father was born again.

What I want to illustrate from this story is that if it had not been for my father's repentance, the chain of my grandfather's sins would have been visited on my generation, and they could have been visited upon my sons and my grandchildren. But my father's repentance broke the cycle. By the way, my grandfather was born again when he was in his seventies under the preaching ministry of his son, my father.

Breaking the Cycle of Generations

There is power in repentance. That's the power of fathers. These are spiritual fathers who are heroes. Fathers who know how to repent will give their spiritual sons a repenting way of life that will bring forth more sons and more daughters. They will all know the way of righteousness because the seed that was planted will bring forth a harvest of more heroes in the Kingdom.

When you take to yourself a son, or when you move in obedience to be a son to a spiritual father, you are setting in motion not just one generation of righteousness, but you are setting in motion a blessing that will flow through the family of God to generation after generation.

Notice what is set in motion. Let me give a few examples. Jesus is the Father's Son. He has set in motion generation after generation of righteousness. Consider Moses and Joshua. Moses fathered Joshua into his place of leadership. By fathering Joshua, he set in motion the whole history of the Hebrew nation. Elijah fathered Elisha. Elijah set in motion a whole new anointing of God, and on Elisha came a double portion of the anointing of Elijah. Paul raised up Timothy, and Timothy led the Church to continue on in the ways of God after Paul died. We, like these examples of spiritual fathers, can set into action multiple generations of righteousness.

Chapter 7
Harnessing Maturity

God will give a house to certain men, a place of fatherhood to steward for Him. When God sets a man in a certain position, He gives him a place of responsibility. God then expects that man's followers to live up to the responsibility of raising up other people to assist in the ministry of that house. God expects us to be good stewards of the people He sends into our lives. The word is clear, if you haven't learned how to do something in your own household, you won't know how to do it in the household of God (see 1 Tim. 3:5). So don't try to do something in the household of God if you haven't first done it in your own household. If you are a good steward of your own household, then you have something to give to the household of God.

The Personality of the House

Each house has its own style and personality. The father of the house necessarily expresses himself in the building of that house. Taking an example from the natural, every household may have a different set of patterns concerning getting out of bed each morning. What is the "getting up" pattern in your household? Whatever the process is in your household, your children will bring that same process into their marriages. One of the many discussions your son or daughter will have with his or her spouse will be about why one set of patterns of getting out of bed are followed instead of another. Both may say something like, "Because that is the way we did it in our family." Every house has it own process of getting up, and we bring that and other baggage with us into our marriages.

The same is true spiritually. What are your processes and patterns? Your sons and daughters will become like you. They will carry your likeness. Everyone who knows you will know who your sons are. That's good; they will carry the righteousness that you give to them.

Being a Son Comes Before Being a Father

Most leaders, especially *developing* leaders, understand that their leadership is still developing and incomplete, so they serve willingly in another man's house until God gives them their own house to lead. The prophet, apostle, pastor, teacher, and evangelist will each serve in another man's house before God gives him his own house to lead. You have to be a son before you can be a father. This generation must learn that you can't be father of a house until you have been the son of a house.

> *And He gave some as apostles, and some as prophets, and some as evangelists, and some as pastors and teachers, for the equipping of the saints for the work of service, to the building up of the body of Christ; until we all attain to the unity of the faith, and of the knowledge of the Son of God, to a mature man, to the measure of the stature which belongs to the fulness of Christ.*
>
> Ephesians 4:11-13

What does a mature son who has been raised up in the house look like? It is essential for this principle to be understood. Many young men in the Body of Jesus Christ miss the ways of God for preparing leaders at this point. They want to move into fatherhood before they have been sons.

An illustration from the natural will help us understand how devastating the problem of becoming fathers before learning to be sons can be. Consider the trend toward promiscuity among the youth of our society. Look around in the natural world and you will see children who are having sexual relationships at very early ages. The girls who are 12 and 13 become pregnant to boys who are 12, 13, or 14 years old, boys who would not understand fathering even if they had the privilege of having a good one of their own.

There are great consequences for a young boy in this situation; he now thinks he is a man. He may brag of his "manhood" from having fathered a child. Yet he can't support the child, and he is not responsible enough to work to support the child. He still wants to play games. He still wants to see other girls. He still wants to have his freedom. He is definitely not ready to be a father, and he has not yet learned to be a son.

If that scenario has such devastating consequences in the natural, imagine how disturbing it is in the Kingdom of God. We have young men who want to be fathers in the house when they haven't yet been sons. They have not yet learned how to be under authority. They have not yet learned to take to themselves the genes of the father, receive from him, and operate in his patterns, rather than resisting the ways of the father as old-fashioned. Young men want to take over the house of God before they've been sons.

A son understands first of all, that it is not his place to be a substitue for the father; his place is to represent the father. In the Body of Christ a son who wants to be a father before being a son severely hurts the Body. He becomes a wolf in sheep's clothing, and he will take advantage of his position in the house for his personal glory, rather than fathering the house for God's glory.

A young couple left our church not long ago. They were quite upset because one of our leaders endeavored to give them strong counsel concerning the financial order in their household. It was an absolute mess. An elder in our house endeavored to give them direction in terms of spiritual oversight. He told them, "I will give oversight to you. I will lead you through this mess." They responded, "Oh, great! That would be wonderful." What the young man thought the elder meant was "I will give you the money to get you out of debt."

When they met for their first meeting the elder began to lay out a plan for them to follow. The young man would be responsible to report to him regularly how he was doing in keeping the payment schedule and bringing the appropriate pattern of righteousness into his finances so his wife would know the security of God in the household and God would be honored by his stewardship. The young man was upset that he wasn't simply getting the money from the elder, and he didn't like being told what he ought to do. He did not want to follow the plan, so he became angry and left our church.

Recently I ran into this young man and his wife at a pastoral gathering. You could have knocked me over with a feather. He greeted me with a big hug and a great big "Praise the name of the Lord." I asked him, "What are you doing here?" He said, "Bless God, I'm the assistant pastor at 'such and such' a church. Come on, meet my pastor." I thought, *Oh, God, he's a leader of men and he has not been a son in spirit and heart. He hasn't learned to be a son yet, but someone is "letting him be a father in the house."* You see spirit ministers to spirit, and in that house, in everything that young man does, he is planting seeds of independence and unsubmissiveness, which will bring forth a harvest of rebellion that will destroy that house. You can't be a father until you've been a son. When you've learned how to be a son, then you can take on the responsibility of fatherhood.

The Integrity of the House

Those who are called to "Ephesians 4" ministries must recognize the integrity of a house and the authority of the father in that house. Often young men and women have a calling on their lives that is genuine, and it has been confirmed by older leaders and by "a sure word of prophecy," but their zeal and excitement causes them to want to step out into ministry prematurely. Young men who know they are called to ultimately serve in that fivefold ministry role of pastor, teacher, evangelist, prophet, or apostle, may see themselves serving in that position before they are ready. They are young men who have not yet learned how to be sons. Yes, they have been called to ultimately take a place of authority, but they have the wrong understanding of the seasons of life.

They desire to take their place of fatherhood in the house and tell everybody what to do and how to do it. The problem is found in their attitude because they have not yet learned how to be a son. The attitude is that an independent spirit often accompanies sonship. They have not yet come under authority and been broken, so they plant the seeds of independence and frustrated anxiety into the Body.

These attitudes breed the same kind of attitudes in others who may also say, "Hurry up and put me in my place. What is my place? I want to serve in this or that leadership role." God is currently raising up mature people who understand the seasons of life. Those who are older (in the Lord, as well as in age) can lead those who are younger into the positions of authority God has chosen for them. The only way they will learn their place is by first being sons and daughters and then being led into position.

The integrity of the house must be kept by those who are being prepared for leadership in the Kingdom. That is why it is so important for those in authority in the house to teach those being prepared that their time of authority is yet to come. Those in authority should give the younger ones opportunity to demonstrate the preparation process in their lives. To whom little is given, little is required. When we are faithful in a little, more is given.

Often young sons want "more" first. This principle can be understood from observing a natural son who endeavors to do more than he is able to do. His inexperience leads to failure. The success mindset of our culture causes us to teach our children that failure is not acceptable, so we press them into adult behavior long before they are ready. And...they continue to fail. We must allow them to be successful as children and teens, so they will be prepared to be successful adults.

This scenario is often repeated in the Kingdom of God because we do not understand the value of the seasons of life. This is an essential ingredient in the spiritual fathering process. God wants to raise up fathers who bring sons into His order. We must teach them by example and give them many opportunities to learn to be successful in doing "little." (See Luke 19:12-26.) When they have been faithful in small things, they will then be prepared for the idea of success in the Kingdom.

God is more interested in maturity than He is in chronological age. The way you mature someone is to teach them how to be successful consistently. Do not put them in a place where they are going to experience failure. Offer opportunities for sure success. Success in submission, obedience, responsibility, and accountability leads to maturity.

As a son matures, offer him opportunity to share what God has put in his heart with a few trusted fathers and sons. Let him be successful. Allow him to experience the blessing and the anointing of God as he brings forth what he has learned. Then give him more to do because he has been faithful in a little.

The Entertainment Syndrome

In the recent history of the church, we suffered from an "entertainment syndrome." Entertainers began getting saved, and two weeks after they were born again we would take them right off the stage and stand them up before a crowd of people as mature believers. We had them give their testimony as though they were paragons of maturity in the Kingdom of God. As a result, these entertainers were often ravished by the devil. In all of its immaturity, the Church of Jesus listened to them as though they were authorities in spiritual development. However, they often spoke as "babes," misinterpreting and misusing Scripture, but it was the best they could do. They were, after all, only spiritual children—definitely not sons, nor fathers.

When you yield to sonship, your motives are purified in the house of God. A good synonym for *sons* is the term "novice." The apostle Paul used this term to refer to those who were not to be allowed into leadership too soon. The entertainers had not been discipled to sonship under spiritual fathers. We lost sight of God's seasons of life. We tried to take shortcuts in God's patterns and seasons, but those shortcuts brought more harm than good. The only way to lay the right foundation for establishing God's Church is for each of us to grow in and through the seasons of life that He has ordained.

Chapter 8

Seasonal Transitions

I have been asked which season for life I consider to be the most difficult. My response is, "All of them." Every season teaches a new dimension of humility, endurance, repentance, and obedience. Each season requires that you learn new applications of these principles.

In every season there are tremendous blessings of God, but there are also those circumstances that make you weep. These are times when you lay on the floor and all you can do is cry in the presence of God. So I would have to say that all of them are my most difficult season *and* my most delightful.

You still have to go through any season you haven't gone through naturally or chronologically. If you have been walking with Jesus for any length of time, you know there are periods of time when God just pushes it all together. It is a form of speed learning. He seems to push it all into a short span of time. Once it's all there, He gives you experiences through which you may apply these truths.

If you are in one season and need to go back to something from a past season, something you didn't experience or you were disobedient in, He will see to it that it is not missed. He wants to prepare us to have quiet lives in each and every season. This is the marvelous grace of God.

The Transitional Role of Fathers

When you look at spiritual fatherhood in the Scriptures, the same father carried the son through all the seasons until he became a father. There is a time when a son becomes a father, and his relationship with his father is no longer the same. Once the son has become a father himself they are on more equal terms. I will tell you how I made this transition naturally with my sons when they became men. I said to them, "When you lived here at home, things were the way your mother and I wanted them. I not only gave you counsel and advice, I gave you orders. You didn't have any choice because it was my household. Now, you will have a choice. I will no longer give you orders. You are a man. Now I am in the place where I will give counsel and advice only when you ask me for it."

It is that way in the spiritual realm. As you become a spiritual son who is moving into spiritual fatherhood, your spiritual father will become your counselor and advisor rather than the one who gives you directions, guidance, and orders. Now you have learned to make decisions for yourself.

It is difficult to be a son who knows that God has called you to a position but also knows that you are not yet ready to take that position. Your spiritual father knows the calling on your life as well. One of the hardest things about being a son is managing the zeal and excitement that is within you.

I use this illustration with young men a lot. A young man is like a young stallion. That stallion has all the potential to be a powerful racehorse, but it is all pent up within him. He does not have any direction for that energy. A stallion, or a herd of stallions, will be grazing happily when suddenly one of them will raise his head. For no reason he will simply run off like the wind in one direction, and all the rest will follow him. They will all run in that direction as fast as they can without knowing where they are going or why they are going there. When they get to wherever it is they were going, they will all begin to graze again. This process may be repeated over and over again. The hardest experience for the stallion is to be captured and brought into a corral where the cowboy begins the slow process of breaking him. This is necessary so a saddle can be placed on his back and a bit in his mouth. This way the stallion can be controlled and directed rather than running off in no particular direction. When the stallion is finally broken he will run in a specific direction with specific purpose because the energy has been harnessed.

The role of the spiritual father is to be God's "cowboy" for bringing the son's will into submission. For the son, the hard part is knowing you have been called, having it burn in your heart, and feeling like you must be turned loose, yet you also know the preparation season is not over. Two things have to happen for that son. First, the father must release him into opportunities in his areas of gifting where he will be successful and not frustrated. He must have the opportunity to learn in areas where he is not filled with anxiety. The son must also continue to be willing to be saddled and bridled. What keeps the anxiety from bursting forth is that the father releases him to ministries that keep him successful. Second, that son must understand that what he may see as being stifled is actually God building humility, endurance, repentance, and obedience in him.

Closing a Season

How do you discern that you're at the end of a season? First, since we naturally live to a certain age, we can mathematically determine approximate transition times from our age. Each 20-year period leads to the next. However, these seasons are not exact so we also have to rely on our own spiritual guidance. You can know you are coming to the end of one season and into the next by the increase of restlessness. It is also wise to rely on the confirming recognition of your spiritual fathers that the transition is taking place.

I have been going through a frustrating transition. My pastor's heart causes me to bear the needs of my spiritual children. For many years the only thing I could do was be a shepherd to my people. I couldn't imagine not being a pastor. It was so important to me. It was my life. It was what made me tick. I loved caring for every single person's need, praying, and making sure the people were cared for and all their needs met. As I have grown in the Lord and in my place in the Kingdom, God keeps pushing me away from this realm of shepherding. I keep holding on to it because it has been my place. Yet God keeps pushing me to a place where I can no longer shepherd in the way I once did it. Now there is a pastoral team, elders, and home group leaders who I shepherd, and they do the shepherding of the people. A transition is in process.

Seasonal Transitions

You know you are at a point of transition when restlessness rises within you, and you feel as though you should be doing something else. Perhaps the old burden is fading to make way for the new season of leadership. God is transitioning you so He can reposition you.

The man is more important than the message. God is never caught by surprise. He is fully aware there may be someone holding you back, even though you feel like it is time for transition. Remember this, God used a donkey to speak His word. He may be using this other person to hold you back. You may think you are ready, but God knows you are not ready yet. The vessel in your way is being used by God to hold you in place until the final character touches are completed for your next season. Yield to it. That's the hard part; because we want to go for it! But if we prematurely go on to the next season it's like the 12, 13, or 14-year-old boy fathering a baby; we will not be ready and our inexperience will provide sure evidence of that fact. God uses His vessels to hold us back until His time.

We were going through a very difficult time in our church. Now I'm submitted to three men outside our church who are like apostolic leaders to me, and through this time I was getting counsel from these three men. It was amazing! I called each one of them and told each one exactly the same thing. They do know each other but they don't live in the same area. They were not conferring with one another, yet every time I called they each gave me the same counsel. During this time of conflict someone sat across from me in a meeting and told me I was anything but a righteous man. He railed on my character and ministry. I was totally devastated! (Understand this: what makes the devil's word so powerful against us is the fact that there is a kernel of truth in it. It has just enough truth for the sensitive heart to say, "I'm guilty of the whole mess" when in fact, we are probably not guilty of it or only partially guilty.) Well, I went to my apostolic leaders and asked them for counsel about the confrontation. Each one gave me exactly the same counsel, "What was said was not true but don't miss the voice of God in it. God wants to talk to you, and He wants to talk to you so desperately that He allowed this mess to be thrown in your face so that you will get on your face and hear Him."

There will be some crossover of the seasons. After feeling stifled, by submitting to leadership you will get your fire back. When you recognize the leadership that is over you, the spiritual father God has put into your life, you will no longer resist their leadership. Every time we walk in obedience, the fire rises again. God is at work in us to will and to do His good pleasure (Phil. 2:13). The Scripture says God resists the proud (Jas. 4:6). So when I rise up in pride, He *must* resist me, He doesn't have a choice because His law, His Holy Word, says He resists the proud. Anything that has pride in it He *has* to resist.

The Scripture says when we walk in resistence to His way, God will resist us. Anytime I rise up in pride, thinking that I have an understanding those who are over me don't quite grasp, I begin to operate somewhat independently. I feel like they have put out my fire, that is when I begin to realize that I am operating in pride. I put out my own fire by my resistance.

The Importance of Transitions

Transitions are critical. Moving from one season of life to another is not as easy as simply deciding to play the next role. However, following the pattern and order of the new season will lead to the blessings God has prepared for that season. The potential of the Church of Jesus Christ depends on whether we will allow ourselves to submit to the processes of each season or if we will demand our own way and hinder the work of God in us.

Everyone has a role in the transitioning process. The son must maintain his submissive ways, even when he believes he is being stifled. The father must be aware of the needs of his son and gradually increase his responsibility so that transitioning can take place. Others must make sure that they do not interfere in the God-ordained process of spiritual fathering.

Chapter 9

Growing Up Fatherless

There are young people within the confines of the Church who are growing up fatherless. Often these young people come from single-parent households where the father is simply not present. Others are from households where the mother is a believer, but the father is not. In these situations the child becomes a spiritual orphan; he is without a spiritual father to guide and direct him from one season of life to the next.

God's Concern

The Scripture clearly shows us that God has a special concern for the fatherless. God understands that even the fatherless need a father to allow passage through the seasons of life. The seasons do not happen automatically. It takes guidance and development in order for the seasons to have the impact God desires.

Moses wrote, "He executes justice for the orphan and the widow, and shows His love for the alien by giving him food and clothing" (Deut. 10:18). God provides for the needs of orphans, whether those orphans are physical or spiritual. He has a loving compassion that extends to practical help. David said, "…Thou hast been the helper of the orphan" (Ps. 10:14) "...He supports the fatherless and the widow..." (Ps. 146:9).

The fatherless hold a special place in God's heart. He looks out for them. He cares for them. He makes sure that each is protected in a way that is befitting of a child of God. This is very different from human understandings of the fatherless. Human beings desire to place blame on others. Often people excuse their own poor behavior by claiming that the other person deserves to suffer because of one action or another. However, God's concern for the fatherless indicates that He takes their needs very seriously. Rather than trying to blame someone for their predicament, the widow and orphan should know that God promises He will be there for them. The fatherless will always find mercy and help from their heavenly Father (see Hos. 14:3).

The Dilemma of the Fatherless

There are many things we take for granted. Having a father in the house provides a sense of identity. Those who have grown up with a father in the house are accustomed to his presence. They know what it is like to interact with their father and receive nurture from him. They know more about their own natures through watching the father that gave them biological life. The father serves as a role model. Little children pretend they are adults in their play in order to learn how to relate in the adult world. They often pretend to be their parents. The father of the house serves as a guide and instructor concerning many different aspects of life and interaction with others. It is from our relationship with our fathers that we best learn how to have deep relationships with others.

The fatherless person misses these things. These same benefits are also missed in the life of the spiritual orphan. Without a spiritual father, a young man does not develop as clear a sense of identity and purpose. A young man without a spiritual father does not have opportunity to model himself after a worthy pattern. He fails to receive proper guidance and instruction. The young man without a spiritual father will fail to see the importance of deep commitments and relationships to others in the Body of Christ.

The fatherless need fathers. The spiritually fatherless need spiritual fathers. Just as growth and development comes through natural interaction in our biological household, so spiritual growth and development comes through the life in our spiritual household of faith. The needs of spiritual orphans must not be overlooked. Instead, Christians must develop the same compassion and concern for the fatherless that God demonstrates in His Word.

A Father to the Fatherless

The Scriptures demonstrate the responsibility of the Church of Jesus to father in the place of a missing father. We are called to provide spiritual fathering over a long period of time. David wrote,

> *A father of the fatherless and a judge for the widows, is God in His holy habitation. God makes a home for the lonely; He leads out the prisoners into prosperity, only the rebellious dwell in a parched land.*
>
> Psalm 68:5-6

The fatherless are a special interest of God's because He intervenes and becomes their father. He replaces their missing father with His own presence, power, and might. He recognizes that the fatherless are lonely and hurting. He knows the hurts and pain they suffer. Therefore, He is willing to make extra sure that the fatherless are cared for.

Human beings interact with one another with their bodies. Words are formed through the mouth, lips, and vocal chords. Hands and feet are necessary to travel and to make gestures. We even recognize one another by our bodies. When we see a familiar face, we know that someone we are acquainted with is present. When God moves on the earth and intervenes in human history, He does so through His Body the Church.

The natural illustrates the spiritual. When God wants to interact with a human being, He usually does so through His body. No doubt He has other means of communication at His disposal, but He prefers to operate through His Body—the Church. When God wants to operate as the father to the fatherless, He wants to use His Body to do so. The Church has the responsibility of being the father of the fatherless.

This can happen in many different ways. One person may take responsibility for a fatherless son in the congregation throughout his seasons and help him through the processes to maturity. The responsibility for the same young man may also be shared by several godly men in the church. The benefit of the group approach is that different men have different understandings and talents to share. One concern with the group approach, however, is that the relationships may not reach the same level of intensity as in the individual father/son process. In either case, the

Word is still clear that the Church must give fathering to the fatherless.

Not only will spiritual orphans benefit as the Church begins to live up to its responsibility as the Body of Christ, but the Church will also benefit. The fatherless have a place in the Kingdom; God has not forsaken them. He prepares the way for them as much as for any other. Since frequently the fatherless have a more difficult time in many aspects of life, they also tend to develop a greater sense of compassion for those who are facing difficulties. The Church needs the contributions these spiritual orphans can make to the Body. However, the only way the Church will benefit from the resource of the spiritually fatherless is by raising them up, not as orphans or illegitimate children, but as complete children of God without any special defect because of their fatherless state.

Part 3

Equipping Young Men

I am writing to you, fathers, because you know Him who has been from the beginning. I am writing to you, young men, because you have overcome the evil one. I have written to you, children, because you know the Father.

1 John 2:13

Chapter 10

One Under Discipline

This chapter is written from the perspective of a young man who has been in the role of a spiritual son to the author. The comments are taken from his public testimony to the benefit of the spiritual father/son relationship.[1]

I feel like the Lord would have me share a little about my past and what He has done. I have found that it is as we are in the position of a son that we learn. Great things happen when we recognize our place as sons. I have also sensed that the Lord would have me share with you concerning the importance of discipline. Let me begin with some history.

I am now 25 years old. My natural parents became divorced when I was eight. Up to that point and following it, my relationship with my father has been less than perfect. Unfortunately, there were also abuses involved. Simply stated, I grew up in a dysfunctional household. I suppose all of us are dysfunctional in one way or another, but the relationship between my natural father and I has definitely been dysfunctional.

---

1. Used by permission.

The Lord is healing my relationship with my natural father, but healing is a process, something that takes time. And it will take time for complete healing in this area. In this process of reconciliation, I don't always understand all the aspects of my relationship to my natural father, but this too is a learning process. God has been more than gracious in providing the proper environment for continual healing to take place.

As I was growing up my relationship with my father was based on fear. Through experiencing various means of intimidation, I felt a lack of self-worth. I understood my father to be someone I feared in a very negative way. There is a healthy fear and an unhealthy fear. An unhealthy fear is based on manipulation and intimidation. Healthy fear is based on respect. My relationship with my natural father was based on unhealthy fear, but God wanted to deal with that negative fear. So the Lord put me with someone who could love me and help destroy the unhealthy fear. God gave me a spiritual father, Pastor Paul Bersche.

Sometimes a son will have many different father types or significant men in his life who will bring changes to him and make him a man of God by building character into his life. I've had several of those kind of men in my life, but Pastor Paul has been the most significant. He is the one who has made the greatest impact in my life. One of the many things that I have learned from Pastor Paul is the meaning of respect and giving him a place of honor in how I approach him and in the way that I serve him. Giving honor and service are characteristics of righteous sonship.

I want you to understand my motivation for being a son. I want to be a son of excellence, and excellence is a process. I had a reputation in the church for being a "nice guy." People would say, "Oh, he always does things right." A friend of mine often jokes with me, saying that I was born with a Bible in my hand and he was born with a cigar in his mouth. In spite of my reputation, I did not truly understand the relationship of Father God with His children. I didn't know what unmerited love was.

Dysfunctional Fatherhood

There are a couple of experiences on my heart I want to share with you. The Lord saw that the fear and apprehension in my life affected my relationship with Him, and He wanted to deal with that. My fear came from my experiences of intimidation and lack of acceptance. I felt that I needed to be performance orientated to gain His acceptance. I felt that if I did things His way He would be happy and then I would be accepted. My natural experiences explain that; when I was a boy I knew that I was okay if I didn't make Dad mad, so if I didn't make Dad mad that meant I was okay. Real issues were never talked about or dealt with because it made Dad happy for me to stay out of his way. That was how I would feel I was okay and accepted.

God didn't want me to be so insecure and crippled inside. The Lord desires openness, honesty, and vulnerability. He wanted to deal with that in me. I'm sharing this because I want you to understand that the Lord will establish spiritual fathers in your life to show you what it means to have a right relationship with God the Father. The ultimate thing the Lord wants to clear up in our understanding is knowing Him as the Father. The Lord brought Pastor Bersche into my life so he could demonstrate to me a love that I never understood before, a love that was there regardless of what I did, what I said, or who I was. I had never known that kind of love.

The Lord used Pastor Paul in many different circumstances to show me this kind of love. In one instance at work, a particularly frustrating and manipulative woman said something that made me very angry. Before I realized it, I just blew up. I was in a hallway and—boom! I punched a door and fractured my hand. I didn't harm the door. It was fine, but, man, that hurt. My hand just throbbed. As the moments passed, I couldn't close my hand due to the swelling. Sure enough, it was broken. Soon after I realized what I did, I went in the men's room and wept. I felt like I had really blown it and that God was very disappointed in me. Once I regained my composure I apologized to the woman and the others around me. Then I went to the doctor.

Sunday was coming and I knew I would see Pastor Paul at church. My experience with my natural father had taught me that making my father upset meant trouble. I knew that if I came into church with this broken hand, or saw Pastor Paul, he would ask, "What happened?" My understanding of a relationship with a father was that he would be disappointed with me. I thought he would say "You blew it. You couldn't handle your anger, and you punched the door. That was wrong. You're bad." Needless to say, I didn't want to tell him. I don't know if you can understand that or not, but that was where I was coming from. I saw the incident as proof that I was a failure. I hadn't done the right thing.

When I told Pastor Paul what happened, I was surprised by his response. He just put his hands on my face

One Under Discipline

and smiled. He said, "That's okay." He accepted me. It went beyond what was sin, what was right, or what was wrong. He accepted me! My relationship with my heavenly Father is the same way. God saw everything. He sees everything that happens in my life. The Lord used Pastor Paul in my life to help me see the way the loving heavenly Father is. It is awesome. It really is awesome.

I feel as though God wants me to challenge you. I am a son, and my experiences are very limited. But what I do have, I want to share. I want you to think about what it was like to be a son or a daughter. What was your relationship with your natural father like? You may not even know your natural father so you may not understand this. You may have had an incredible home life. But the likelihood is that all of us are dysfunctional in some way or another. What was it like when you were raised? What was it like to be a son, or a daughter, growing up—in elementary school, in high school, in junior high? What was it like?

Imagine that picture, the good times, the bad times. Then I want you to lay that down. I want you to look at it the way the Lord says it is. It has been a process, and it is a process in our lives for us to begin to understand what it means to have a true father, a heavenly father, a loving father.

Truth is truth. Truth is what God says. Now we all come into sonship, and even fatherhood, with paradigms. Paradigms are our views, the way we see things based upon our own experiences. I saw a relationship with the father as something that if I did everything right, if I didn't argue, and if I kept things calm, then I would be okay. That is not the way God sees it, however. God wants us to be honest with Him, and He wants us to be honest with our fathers, those that are heads over us. He wants us to learn from them.

I remember one example of how my fear affected my actions. When I was young my dad had an old car. It was falling apart. But my Dad had an anger problem. When things weren't going right, he would get upset, yell, hit, or whatever. Once my sister and I were in the front seat while dad was driving. The door next to me began to rattle and make noise. Dad started to get upset. My first reaction was, "I don't want Dad mad." I grabbed the door and held it close to myself so it would make less noise. There was so much fear involved. I felt responsible for the noise that door made. That was my way of thinking, and it was natural for me to think that way.

I'm sure there are things in your life that the Lord is revealing to you about ways you relate to the Father. Are they really based on truth? Are you doing things, are you relating to God the Father, the way He wants you to? I really want to encourage you. Let the Lord speak to you. We are all in places of change. We're all learning what it means to be sons. There are different levels. You become a father naturally and you become a father spiritually, but it is a process.

The Good of Discipline

Once you realize your sonship and begin to submit to the authority that God has set up over you, the Lord will begin to teach you about discipline. He wants to make us disciples through a paradigm of discipline. Discipline often seems negative. As a kid growing up, your mom or dad would say, "Don't do that! Put that down! Get out of there! What are you doing?" We see that as being disciplined. We look at it from a negative perspective. We tend to look at godly or "heavenly Father" discipline the same way: "I couldn't get that"; "I wasn't able to receive that"; "I've got to wait for that."

The Lord wants to show us how discipline needs to be viewed. It means God wants you to experience the fullness of all He has for you. How's that for a new twist? Discipline is a good thing. Think about playing basketball or other sports. If you are disciplined at a sport, you become good at it. Discipline requires pain, endurance, and at times, even humility. Discipline is a good thing. Our paradigm needs to be switched.

The Lord has used Pastor Paul naturally in disciplining me. I remember asking for his advice about dating. I would say, "Hey, what do you think about her? Maybe I should start dating her. What do you think about that?" He would say, "Oh, my son...." Then he would begin asking questions to help me. A father knows how to ask the right questions. It's amazing the thoughts that he can encourage in me—ways of thinking that I wouldn't have considered otherwise. He helps with money issues as well. I would ask, "I like that car. What do you think about me buying it?"

"Well, can you afford it?"

"No."

"All right then."

That was the bottom line, no. He has a way of not telling me what to do, but giving me just enough hints and questions to create the wisest choice within me.

A maturing process occurs as a son begins to recognize that Dad knows what he is talking about. He is not 40, 50, or 60 years old without purpose. He has been through what I am going through. He has asked the same questions. The Lord has set up the Church and the natural family so that wisdom and insight come from above you. If you, as a son or a daughter, don't know what the Lord's will is in a situation, you can trust God to tell your father—your spiritual father. That's the order God has set up to help you get through life. Take advantage of it. Find a father to get under and God will set all that out. Let the Lord set it up.

God's desire to fulfill goals and vision in you is stronger than your own. But God won't bless you nor give you that anointing until you're prepared for it. God's design is for you to get there as fast as you can. Speed is basically determined on your obedience. How fast are you willing to submit, to yield, to change, to be the man or woman of God that He wants you to be?

One of the things I have learned about discipline and the ways of God is that God will do what He's going to do whether you like it or not. My prayer from the heart, even when the emotions weren't there, has been, "God, I want Your best. I want Your very best. I don't want to settle for second best." The Lord has blessed me with a drive to pursue excellence, to do the right thing. I'm far from being perfect, but I'm pursuing excellence. The Lord has designed the circumstances of your life, and when you are wholly submitted to Him, you will be put in circumstances that you won't understand. You will even be put into circumstances that you won't necessarily enjoy.

Remember the place where I broke my hand? I was promoted to mill supervisor. I had five or six guys under my supervision. The co-owners at the time were going to sell the business. I approached them and said, "I want to buy it." I was 22 at the time. I had financial backing behind me. I was being responsible as a manager and making really good money. I even had a new silver sports car and a girlfriend. But I was a son. At the time I believed with all my heart I was in that business as a form of ministry. I intended to bring in guys who didn't have work discipline and train them up. I thought that was what God was doing.

Then the company began to experience some financial problems; they laid some people off. I was one of those people. During this time there was some friction between the owners and myself. There was a manipulative Jezebel spirit in the company, and a lot of illegal things were going on. At that time I thought, *Well, Lord, I think it's time for me to leave and move on.* I was laid off for eight months. I didn't understand what was going on. I questioned whether the Lord really wanted me at that company owning it and running it as a ministry. I had my college degree. In fact, I finished school on Thursday and was laid off on Friday. I thought, *No, this isn't supposed to happen like this.*

I sought the Lord, "God, what are you doing?" I had no understanding of what the Lord was doing, but the Lord orchestrated everything perfectly, even though I did not understand what He was doing. In a nutshell, through that time of searching and thinking I understood God, there was a discipline process happening. As far as I was concerned, I was powerless to change my circumstances. I could have gone and worked at a fast food place or something. I could have found another job, but there was a place the Lord wanted me. I needed to get my significance from Him.

The only way I was able to find that special place was to have things taken from me. Saul received his anointing and kingship before he had the necessary life experiences to be king. And you saw what happened to his kingdom. David was trained through hellish experiences; he was chased, beaten, starved, and had his family possessions taken. Then he returned to become king of Israel. Discipline is an important process for us.

So, I had a sports car, girlfriend, and a good income. I thought I was ready and had everything in order. I planned to make lots of money for God. I was going to do the right thing. Then all of a sudden, I was laid off, broke up with the girlfriend, and lost the car. I couldn't find work, went into debt, and lost it all, everything. But there is hope. After the eight-month layoff, some friends of mine hired me to work in a computer company. I was brought on to do a lot of routine administrative things. I was an "office manager." That's a colorful way of saying you're a secretary/receptionist. I expected to only be there for a month or so. I've been there for about a year now, and I'm still doing the same thing. I was asking, "God, what are you doing? What are you doing with my life? I don't understand."

The Lord spoke to me, "Where are you getting your significance? Who are you looking to?" If the Lord had let me own that business, have that sports car, girlfriend, and everything else, would I have learned that lesson? Would I know where I was getting my significance? Would I know what it means to have a loving father? My dependence would be on myself, I wouldn't have any need for the Lord, for the Father. God wanted to deal with that.

There is a sense of humility in my life now. I'm a secretary. I have a college degree. What's the deal? I'm answering phones, sending faxes, and making copies. I don't get it, I've got a four-year college degree. I may think, *A plus B is not equalling C here*, but it is. There are good things happening in my life. I know I am in the Lord's hands. He is changing my paradigm.

The Scripture provides instructions concerning talking to older men as fathers, brothers, and younger men as sons. Listen to what the Lord is doing in your life. Don't belittle the place you are in; it is the place the Lord has brought you to. As a son, I'm not at the place of fulfillment. I am a learner. I thought I was fulfilled and making my mark on the Church and the world. Then everything crashed and fell apart. Now God is building it up the way it should be. If I had received all the blessings and anointing back then, I would not have what the Lord really wanted to do. But since I have made a choice to submit and to say, "Yes, Lord," and, "Yes," to my spiritual father, He's going to take me places; He's going to show me things; He's going to reveal things to me that I never knew before about myself.

As a son, you will make a lot of mistakes. That's part of the deal. It's a process. There was a time when I thought,

I'd like to be a pastor. I want to lead people. Someday I want to be an elder in the church and in the forefront. Throughout this two-year season, I haven't wanted to have anything to do with leading people. My attitude has been "No way, get me out of here; I don't think I want to do that—a lot of headaches, a lot of people problems." But in time, the Lord saw to it that I was asked to be a part of leadership. He said, "I think you're ready now. I think you're ready to lead a home fellowship group." We have between 12 and 20 people in our home group. I'm one of the younger ones, but the Lord is doing some incredible things.

God's ways are not our ways. He saw to it that my character was developed through some circumstances so I would be prepared for this place. I am very glad I am here now. It's not easy, but I know I have the Lord's blessing and His timing, and I wouldn't trade that for anything. I really wouldn't. So, keep going, keep going! Submit to the Lord, His ways, and His discipline. If you don't understand it, you know, that's okay; that's part of the deal. You're not supposed to understand all of the time.

Chapter 11

Five Keys to Fathering

It is essential for understanding Scripture and God's ways to first and foremost see God as Father. If you don't understand Scriptures the way God has intended, if you are going to have more than mere knowledge of the ways of God, then you *must* see that God has written the Bible as the ultimate expression of the love of the Father to His children.

It is not easy to discuss fatherhood in today's society. Often folks have such a poor image of their earthly father that they have difficulty making the transfer from their understanding of their earthly, natural father to seeing God as the Father. They simply view God the same way they see their natural father. However, as the healing work of God takes place in our lives, we can look beyond the natural father and see the fathering work of God that begins the process of acceptance. The fathering work of God is filled with grace, lots of love, and mercy.

We must begin to view what God does from His viewpoint and His standard of doing things. His work is full of grace. He gives us His unmerited favor, rather than being an iron-fisted authoritarian who wounds and slaps people around—hurting them with words as well as with fists. In order to understand what God is saying, we have to ask Him to help us see that He is first and foremost the Father.

Remember, time is God's way of keeping everything from happening at once. The good news is that even though you can't do everything at once, you still get to do just about everything, one season at a time. One of the problems with sons is they want to do everything in the first 20 years. When my oldest son finished high school, he worked with a young man who owned a little business. On a daily basis, that young man would complain, "I'm 27 years old and I'm not a millionaire yet." He had grown up believing he had to be extremely successful at a very young age. His self-worth and security were connected to his wealth, or lack of wealth. What a shame!

If you are willing to walk in God's time pattern, in the fullness of time you will get to do everything. You will do it one season at a time, with fewer failures, more successes, and no regrets. If Jesus was brought forth in the fullness of time, you can count on the fact you also will be brought forth in the fullness of time. He will not ignore you or your place. You are very important to Him.

God Places Fathers and Sons

Spiritual fathering is a process of leading sons through the seasons of life and releasing them to their place of leadership in God's Kingdom. God designed the placement of fathers and sons in the Body. He places, and He appoints. The Father God brings into your life (or if you are a father, the son He will bring into your life to take under your wing) will greatly be determined by your placing. In other words, you are not in the church that you are in by your own choice. It was divine choice. God brought you to that place. He has placed you, He has appointed you there for sonship, for discipleship, and for blessing. You have to recognize you are not where you are by your own doing. The nudging and directive work of God have put you where you are so that you can come under sonship, discipleship, and blessing. This is a key factor in the working of God.

Fathering is for raising leaders through sonship. Discipling is for raising many believers into strong disciples. Blessing is for the multitudes. Jesus blessed the multitudes, gathered a few around Him for strengthening and discipleship, and He raised up 12 for leadership (sonship). Jesus did not talk about family issues to the multitudes. He kept the intimate matters for those closest to Him. He only talked of family issues with His sons, His disciples.

Your placement—where you live in your town, where you live in your community, where you work, and where you go to church, the believers God has connected you to—is not by your choice. Those were the choices of God. You have been *put* in those places so that God can bring you into place of sonship, discipleship, and blessing.

When you wrestle against where God has put you, you wrestle against the sonship, discipleship, and blessing God wants to bring on you. Often when things do not happen exactly as we would like them to in our neighborhood, in our church setting, in our work setting, or in our educational setting, we simply run away. That is one of our first responses here in America. We learn the patterns that are simplest at the moment without thinking about later consequences. When we do not like something, we run away from it. It is an American pattern. We run from our education, or go to another university. At work, we run from what we don't like. If we don't like the neightborhood we're in, we move to another neighborhood. If we don't like government in our community, we move to another community. If we don't like the church we are in, we will move to another church. After all, it's just the American way; you don't deal with the issues, you just move.

We have forgotten that God is at work to will and to do His good pleasure (Phil. 2:13), to bring us into sonship, discipleship, and great blessing. This is the order of God. Placement has a great deal to do with coming under the leadership of a father. If you are a father, it has to do with bringing you into place with sons who will follow your leadership.

There are Many Influences, But Few Fathers

Not everyone who has input into your life is a father. God provides a variety of people to influence us in different ways. We have many needs, and our God is careful to see that those needs are met. The people God places in our lives have a variety of roles and functions, and they are worthy of a variety of levels of respect. In order to best operate and interact with those around us, we must take care to recognize the level of authority we should give to each person God places in our path.

In First Corinthians 4:15, Paul says there are tutors, or schoolmasters, who are important in life. They instruct us about repentance. In Galatians 4:1 and following, Paul speaks of guardians. You will have tutors and guardians who will show you the way to repentance. In First Timothy 3,

Paul spoke about managers who will show you the way to manage your own household. They will show you how to manage your life, business, children, and household. Understand that not everyone has the place of a father in your life. There are tutors; there are guardians; and there are managers. Managers show us how to execute the law of the house in which we live. If we are the one over the house, then we must execute the law that we give to the house. This is very important. (Again, not everyone who has input into your life is a father.)

Do not live with expectations that cannot be met. One of the problems in marriage, as well as in other kinds of relationships, is that we all enter into our relationships with expectations that we have not communicated to the other person. This happens in churches. Folks come into a church, but they don't communicate their expectations to the church. Similarly, the church does not communicate its expectations to the people who attend. We live with the continual concern of whether we are meeting the other person's requirements.

One of the most important issues that I share with a young couple before they are married is regarding expectations: "What are your expectations of this person who is going to be your spouse?" I ask them to write down some things: "What do you expect him to be and to do as your husband? What do you expect of this woman? Let's write down those things so they can be communicated now to your spouse." When people are married there are really six people standing there at the altar. There is the woman the bride really is, the woman she *thinks* she is, and the woman *he* thinks she is. There is also the man the groom really is, the man he *thinks* he is, and the man *she* thinks he is. So we are dealing with a huge amount of expectations that are unknown because they are uncommunicated.

We must start talking about what those expectations are so that they can either be met together or we can agree to change them. Even if they are not expressed, it is likely we will know we are not meeting the expectations of our spouse or friend. Then a great deal of energy will be expended trying to determine what those expectations are, defending one's self against those expectations, or in trying to meet them and always failing. That is very demoralizing. Each one knows there are some unsatisfied or unresolved areas in the other's life, but neither of them know what they may or may not do to resolve the dilemma. Without this knowledge, each of them aims to satisfy the other. However, the aim and the uncommunicated expectation rarely match. Each one knows he or she has missed again, but he has no idea what it is he missed. If by chance he happens to meet the unknown expectation right on, it still doesn't satisfy the other one because immediately, without desiring to be difficult, the uncommunicated standard is unexpectedly raised.

When we don't know what the expectations are, we can't meet them. This creates tremendous frustration. Everyone who has input into your life isn't a father; they may be a tutor, a guardian, or a manager who may assist you with specific areas of your life. Give to each the authority, honor, and respect due their position. Still recognize the person is not your father. The father's role includes these ministries, but it goes beyond them to also include heart development.

Authority and Discipline

Not everyone who influences your life is a father. The spiritual father has a relationship of authority and discipline with the son. He is one who calls you to order. He's the one with the grace to say, "Look, you're going to buy this car? Let's sharpen the pencil and see if the numbers make sense." The father's figures may reach a different sum than the son's figures because of the father's years of experience and wisdom.

Spiritual fathering couples authority and discipline with a grace that allows the son to make decisions for himself. Sometimes the father will have to let a son crash and burn. Sometimes we learn better when we crash and burn. But it is vital to not let the son burn up and be destroyed. As the fire of discipline begins, the father must come alongside to be the encourager during that burning discipline of God.

Discipline is accomplished by yielding to the authority that is over us in the Lord. In the eyes of Jesus, faith is developed out of authority and discipline. There's a story in Matthew of a centurion who came to Jesus because he had a sick servant. He said, "I know what it's like to be under authority, so you don't need to come to my home. Just say the word. I understand authority, so I know it will be done. I am a man under authority myself, and I understand the principle." Jesus recognized his faith and said, "Your servant is well." (See Matthew 8:5-13.)

Jesus explained that this centurion had the greatest faith He had seen in all of Israel. His faith was in effect because he understood authority, and authority is filled with grace and discipline. So faith is increased by being under authority and discipline. As a son, in that place of authority and discipline, we learn to serve those who are over us in the Lord. God intended our lives to be marked by servanthood. We learn it best by serving a father's gifts and vision. This is faith. Faith is the key to operating in the power of the spirit of God. It is developed by our willingness to be under authority and discipline.

Service and Dependence

A spiritual father's purpose is to develop the son's dependence on the Holy Spirit. In the heart of a natural father who is a committed believer, there is a longing flowing from the Father-heart of God within him to build into his children an attitude of dependence upon the Holy Spirit. From very early in our children's lives, we can teach them to depend upon the Spirit of God and have a servant's heart.

Paul wrote to the Philippian church,

Make my joy complete by being of the same mind, maintaining the same love, united in spirit, intent on one purpose. Do nothing from selfishness or empty conceit, but with humility of mind let each of you regard one another as more important than himself; do not merely look out for your own personal interests, but also for the interests of others.
Philippians 2:2-4

We must be about the business of asking, "How can I serve you? What is it that you need?" Once we find a need, it is the responsibility of fellow believers to meet that need or to find others who can help meet that need. In the Body of Jesus Christ, the spiritual father endeavors to teach his spiritual sons and daughters to develop a dependence upon the Spirit of God and build into them a servant's heart.

How do you build servanthood and dependence on the Spirit of God? You build it by modeling it. You build it by doing it with your son or daughter. In the midst of a situation you teach your son how to depend upon the Spirit of God by depending on Him for your own needs. Teach your son or daughter how to be a servant *by serving them*, the older serving the younger.

The order of the world is that the younger serves the older. The order of the world is that the lesser serves the greater. It has always been that way in the corporate structure; the lesser serves the greater. Jesus said, "I don't do things like corporate America." Jesus is not an American. He stands alone as the King of His own Kingdom. He said we are not to live according to the patterns of the world. We are going to learn how to do things by the elder serving the younger, the greater serving the lesser; then the lesser will know how to serve the greater. This is why Jesus washed the feet of the disciples. This upset Peter, for he understood the corporate world—"I'm lesser; You are greater!" But Peter did not understand that the way of the Kingdom of God contradicts the world.

But Jesus called His disciples to Him and said,

...You know that the rulers of the Gentiles lord it over them, and their great men exercise authority over them. It is not so among you, but whoever wishes to become great among you shall be your servant, and whoever wishes to be first among you shall

> *be your slave; just as the Son of Man did not come to be served, but to serve, and to give His life a ransom for many.*
>
> Matthew 20:25-28

This is the will of the Father. We must teach the way of servanthood and dependence on the Spirit of God. Jesus gave His mind, emotions, will, drive, vision, and purpose to those who were following Him. In the process of teaching us dependence and a servant's heart, Jesus paid the price to set me free from the ways of the world. He paid our ransom. This is what the Father has done. What is in the heart of the natural father is also experienced by the spiritual father. We recognize that we pay a ransom to free another person to take his place in the Body of Jesus Christ.

A price is paid to gain the son's release from where he is into the place God has planned for him. Spiritual fathering in the Kingdom of God requires discernment and commitment to recognizing young men and women who need to be ransomed. We must lay down our will, emotions, mind, vision, and purpose to bring these young people into their place in the Kingdom of God.

Immediately, the American mind says, "What about me?" Let me assure you that as you give yourself to bring a young man into his place in the Kingdom of God, God will see to it that you will know your place. There is no need to be concerned about that. When you have the privilege of ransoming other men into their place through laying down your life, you will see it is worth the price. Laying down your life means giving away your time, the time you would ordinarily have kept for yourself. Believe me it is worth the price.

The concept of "laying down my life" is not an ethereal theory. It is simply giving of the time I would spend on myself (or time I had planned to use differently) to someone else to pay the price for them to find their place. This is the stuff that natural and spiritual fathering in the household of God is all about. These issues, related to this realm of dependence on the Spirit of God and building servanthood, were spoken by Jesus to His *disciples*, not to the multitudes.

The Sermon on the Mount was really for the disciples. When Jesus spoke of the Kingdom and Kingdom matters, that was household stuff. He didn't tell family secrets to the multitudes. In every home there are countless issues that parents choose not to discuss with their children. Perhaps the children are not yet able to bear the load of this knowledge. Many of these issues are financial, emotional, or concern planning for the future. These are kept in the home. The failings of our family members are not to be aired to the whole community like dirty laundry. Instead, private issues are to be kept private for the sake of the integrity of the home.

Jesus *demonstrated* the Kingdom to the multitudes, but He *taught* about Kingdom issues with His disciples, those that were closest to him. These were His sons, His disciples in ministry. As fathers, we need to give away the things God has been putting into our hearts as we have grown in Him. We put those things into our sons and daughters by walking in the way with them. Fathers should not end up preaching sermons. Fathers must be committed to ministering to the needs of the children. That's how the training process works; the spiritual father demonstrates God's ways throughout his life. He teaches as the need arises, but he demonstrates how the truth is applied by living it himself and expecting the sons to follow.

Inheritance Belongs to the Sons

Only a son can inherit. You and I are sons of God, and it is our privilege to inherit the Kingdom of God. Sons inherit from the father, naturally and spiritually. We inherit all kinds of things from our father. We take on his thought processes, his ways, and his principles. As we grow in sonship we also add ways of our own. My spiritual father gave me his principles, attitudes, and patterns of thinking, as did the man who was both my natural and spiritual father. To these I added my own. During the growing process I discarded some of my own attitudes and patterns and took on all they offered that was godly. They are now a part of me. Neither you nor I can ever differentiate between their lives and mine. For better or for worse, I am who they and God have made me to be. That is exactly what happens when a son is in relationship with a spiritual father over a period of time. He begins to inherit his father's life.

An impartation takes place from father to son. Unfortunately, the son receives both strengths and weaknesses through the father/son relationship. The son has to learn how to eat the meat and throw out the bones. That too is part of the training process.

There is an impartation of the father's patterns of thinking, reactions to life, and personal perspectives. There is an impartation of principles and the practical application of the truth of God to real life situations. There is also an imparting of vision. By imparting his own vision, the father opens the mind and the spirit of the son to allow the spirit of God to impart to the son a vision of his own. Left to himself, the son's vision would be very narrow and restricted. However, when given the heavenly Father's vision *and* the expanse of the spiritual father's vision the son's mind and heart are opened to something far beyond what he could ever imagine for himself. This is what inheriting is all about.

Only a son can inherit. God has promised that we will inherit the earth. He was not talking about the ways of the earth, He was explaining that we inherit all that is godly in heaven and earth. "For the earth is the Lord's and the fulness thereof" (1 Cor. 10:26 KJV). Sons who are meek in spirit inherit all that belongs to the father, so it takes meekness to be an inheritor. The inheritance comes to meekness—not weakness, but meekness. The gentle, serving son who learns how to serve his father in the midst of all his fire and fury experiences the wonderful privilege of inheriting all that belongs to God.

God gives us the privilege of inheriting much. Not only does this truth relate to spiritual fathering, but it also relates to our entire relationship with Father God. We are addressing issues in our relationship to Father God and His relationship to us that have application to spiritual fathering and sonship, which, in turn, have application to natural fathering and sonship. They all have the same pattern.

Indeed, God has provided us with keys to spiritual fathering to make sure we understand these truths. We need to walk in them with a fervency that will shake the world and change the future. The power and anointing that is passed from one generation to the next has a multiplying effect so long as there are people who are willing to give themselves as spiritual fathers and those who are willing to be sons and submit to and accept the leadership of their fathers. The responsibility falls to both sides of the relationship. One cannot happen without the other. As we apply these keys to spiritual fathering, we begin to determine the direction of future generations in a marvelous way. Every answer we need is provided for us in His book, the Bible. Fathers, give to your sons. Sons, receive from your fathers and give yourselves to them.

Part 4

Fathers and Mentors

Paul, an apostle of Christ Jesus by the will of God, according to the promise of life in Christ Jesus, to Timothy, my beloved son: Grace, mercy, and peace from God the Father and Christ Jesus our Lord. I thank God, whom I serve with a clear conscience the way my forefathers did, as I constantly remember you in my prayers night and day, longing to see you, even as I recall your tears, so that I may be filled with joy. For I am mindful of the sincere faith within you, which first dwelt in your grandmother Lois, and your mother Eunice, and I am sure that it is in you as well. And for this reason I remind you to kindle afresh the gift of God which is in you through the laying on of my hands. For God has not given us a spirit of timidity, but of power and love and discipline.

2 Timothy 1:1-7

Chapter 12

Moses and Joshua

The Scripture provides us with several wonderful examples of ministry being passed from one generation to the next. When we look at biblical history, we cannot ignore how God passed the mantle and anointing of ministry from one person to another. The first example of that passing of ministry is found in the story of Moses and Joshua. Joshua, the son, inherited Moses' ministry. Exodus 24:13 reads, "So Moses arose with Joshua his servant, and Moses went up to the mountain of God."

Joshua received his impartation from Moses over the years. In fact, the Scriptures teach that Joshua was Moses' servant. He spent 15 years in Moses' tent caring for all his needs. Moses gave Joshua the same ministry that God had given to him. Joshua was Moses' servant. He took care of Moses' practical needs. Because he was around Moses on a consistent basis, he picked up Moses' traits and attributes. He grew in his ability to deal with issues the way Moses dealt with issues. Joshua received from Moses by serving him and being in his presence in the midst of the requirements of every day leadership.

The son is confirmed to the people by the father. What takes place in the order of God when a Moses gives his ministry to a Joshua? When the son is prepared and the father is prepared, the work of the Spirit in their lives will reveal it is time for the ministry to be transitioned. This is when the son is confirmed before the people by the father.

You may remember Deuteronomy 31:7 when Moses stood before the people to confirm that Joshua was being prepared to be their leader. I believe in this concept. If, for example, I speak to a roomful of pastors, I admonish them to pray for God to give them a Joshua who will one day move into their place of ministry. At that point they will be able to stand him before the people and confirm that young man's life and ministry. Then when God, by His divine processes, removes the father from the place, there is no delay in the process of the workings of God because the new leader has already been established.

I personally believe that pulpit search committees are an ungodly process established by the world and adopted by the Church. We have endeavored to "sanctify" the "headhunting" pattern of the world. It is like trying to transplant a head onto a body. The truth is, a head transplant doesn't work. In the case of a church, the body often rejects the new head. Very often the body will simply not connect with the new head well enough to listen to his instructions and leadership.

We do not prepare leaders very well to take over in the church. The corporate world and government seem to have a better plan. If something happens to a leader in these realms, a vice president takes over. He is prepared by the leader to lead, and he is confirmed before the people (the board) as the man who is the heir apparent when the current leader is removed. As the next person in line to be president, he gets caught up in the process of the governmental machinery. Once in place, the new person must learn the process of being a leader. Even though he may be prepared corporately, politically, and governmentally the strength of his heart qualities will still remain somewhat untested. Now, in the Church we should be modeling the thing we do best—heart preparation—along with governmental training. The impartation of those internal qualities is what prepares a man to be the leader God has chosen.

My understanding of this issue in the Scriptures is that when the pastor, the shepherd-leader, is gone, the people should hardly notice because the presence of God and the order of the house continues unabated because the father's pattern has been previously established. It is very encouraging to return from having been away and find my church has done quite well without me. It is also a valuable lesson in humility that God uses to keep us recognizing that it is His Church, and His leaders do quite well without us.

Moses prepared the people to one day receive Joshua as their leader. Moses stood Joshua beside him, made a declaration to the people, and confirmed it. We must also notice how the father passes the anointing to the son. Through Joshua spending those 15 years in Moses' tent and through their personal relationship, Moses imparted his anointing for leadership upon Joshua. Joshua stood with him as he made decisions. Joshua met with him when the elders met to pray. When the 70 elders went to the mountain to pray for the people of God, Joshua was a part of that group. When the leaders gathered around Moses to make decisions about the advancement of Israel as they moved across the wilderness, Joshua was always sitting in.

It is interesting to note that although Joshua was in Moses' tent, which implies he was part of the governmental decision making process, you never hear of Joshua having input. His silence is important. He was receiving and gleaning from all the older men around him, learning to lead God's way. Moses was imparting his anointing to him.

> *Now Joshua the son of Nun was filled with the spirit of wisdom, for Moses had laid his hands on him; and the sons of Israel listened to him and did as the Lord commanded Moses.*
> Deuteronomy 34:9

Another important aspect from the relationship of Moses and Joshua is the son works alongside the father for a season. Joshua worked alongside Moses for 15 years. A lot of young men think they are ready long before their preparation time is completed. But this is a process of God. He knows the importance of timing. It is so important for us to understand the seasons of God. The seasons were essential for preparing Joshua to transition his thinking from anticipating "my ministry" to thinking of it as "God's ministry."

A son may be in prayer before the Lord when the anointing of God comes upon him, the Word speaks rhema truth to him, and revelation begins to rise up in him. The son will begin to see himself in the order of God in the future. He will know what he is supposed to do and who he is supposed to be, how he is to live and move and have his being in God. He will see his place in the Kingdom of God. It will be confirmed by other spiritual leaders. After it has been prophesied and confirmed, he will begin to dream—"my ministry, wow!" His eyes become glassy and he begins to take himself too seriously, "My ministry, look out world! Wow, my ministry. I can just see the multitudes coming to God, being healed, delivered, blessed, encouraged, and set free. Turn me loose!" But he is still thinking "my ministry." So God must take the time necessary to break him from the thoughts of "my ministry" to understand God's ministry.

Moses had been in the ministry a long time, he was past 80 when Joshua lived in his tent. Moses had been "down the road," and he understood God's ways. He understood the hardships and blessings of the ways of God. He understood that when God pours out anointing for leadership the leader cannot be thinking of making any claim whatsoever to his own greatness because he knows that God is the only one who has any claim to greatness because it is His in the first place.

The transition will begin to demonstrate itself in the vocabulary of the young man. He will begin to delete talk of "my ministry." Instead he will speak of the ministry of the Kingdom of God and the ministry of the Church of Jesus Christ. He will think and speak of the ministry of the Holy Spirit. When I hear the words "my ministry" I know there is still some training yet to be done; in the Kingdom of God there is no "my ministry." "My ministry" indicates the author of Lordship is not completely settled in that young man's heart.

I am concerned about what is happening in the Body of Christ regarding the lack of need for faith. The current mixture of psychology and the Word of God says that you must understand yourself, so we appear to be building a church that is more concerned with contemplating our own navels in order to find and understand ourselves than in giving ourselves to God. As long as you are trying to find yourself, you will not find God. The Word is clear: Seek first the Kingdom of God, and all these things shall be added unto you (see Mt. 6:33).

As long as my concern is knowing myself, I am the lord of my life. My understanding of the people, the circumstances, and the plans I have for my life all become enthroned. When I'm seeking Him, then His ways and His plans are enthroned. Moses imparted God's life to Joshua. When they went into battle, there were times Moses gave Joshua opportunities to lead. He said, "You go and surround the city from one side, I will surround them from the other. They will think I am the only one coming, and they will run right into your lap so you can capture them." Joshua was given those opportunities of leadership so Moses could transfer his ministry into the hands of Joshua. Anytime Joshua tried to own it for himself, God dealt with him about it.

There will always be a time of commissioning.

Then He commissioned Joshua the son of Nun, and said, "Be strong and courageous, for you shall bring the sons of Israel into the land which I swore to them, and I will be with you."
                                    Deuteronomy 31:23

Once the commissioning takes place, there is the divine removal of the father. In this case, the divine removal of the father was that Moses walked off into the mountains and God buried him. Isn't that incredible? God buried Moses. Then Joshua, the son, inherited the full responsibility of leading the people of God.

Although the lessons we can learn from Moses and Joshua are still tremendous, we need to turn our attention now to Elijah and Elisha.

Chapter 13

Elijah and Elisha

In the model of Moses and Joshua, there was the giving of Moses' ministry to Joshua. In the model of Elijah and Elisha, there is the giving of the gift, the mantle, rather than the giving of the ministry. I believe Elijah exemplifies the gifting of service as well as any figure in the Scriptures. Elijah models the key to fathering through giving the serving process to Elisha. There was a season of serving as Elisha learned the positives and negatives of the gift of prophecy. Matthew 20:28 reads, "Just as the Son of Man did not come to be served, but to serve, and to give His life a ransom for many." The whole process of serving is persistence in the gift. Persistence in the gift is always tested. Will you keep on serving under all circumstances? Elisha was put in the squeeze. Would he persist in serving under any circumstance? Your gift will always be tested.

> *And it came about when the Lord was about to take up Elijah by a whirlwind to heaven, that Elijah went with Elisha from Gilgal. And Elijah said to Elisha, "Stay here please, for the Lord has sent me as far as Bethel." But Elisha said, "As the Lord lives and as you yourself live, I will not leave you." So they went down to Bethel. Then the sons of the prophets who were at Bethel came out to Elisha and*

said to him, "Do you know that the Lord will take away your master from over you today?" And he said, "Yes, I know; be still." And Elijah said to him, "Elisha, please stay here, for the Lord has sent me to Jericho." But he said, "As the Lord lives, and as you yourself live, I will not leave you." So they came to Jericho. And the sons of the prophets who were at Jericho approached Elisha and said to him, "Do you know that the Lord will take away your master from over you today?" And he answered, "Yes, I know; be still." Then Elijah said to him, "Please stay here, for the Lord has sent me to the Jordan." And he said, "As the Lord lives, and as you yourself live, I will not leave you." So the two of them went on.

2 Kings 2:1-6

It seems Elijah purposely put Elisha in the place where he had to be willing to lay himself down for his spiritual father. The test was clear: "I am going over here, you stay here." Elisha says "Oh, no, you're not leaving me." In each new location, Elisha was being tested. Will the servant purchase the gift by the laying down of his soul. What is the soul? The mind, emotions, and the will. Will he lay down what he thinks? Will he lay down how he wants to feel? Will he lay down what he wants to decide?

Elijah took Elisha first to Gilgal. Gilgal means "the place of rolling away the circumcision of the heart." Is he going to be willing to pursue the gift God has put within him? Then they went to Bethel. Once again Elijah said, "You stay here now." Elisha responded, "Oh, no, I'm persistent in my service to you, I'm going to follow you. I will stay with you to serve you." This was God's testing of Elisha to see if he was going to lay down his self. You know, many of us get to the place where God works the circumcision of our heart within us and then we become self-satisfied; "Well, I yielded and passed the test so I will use my gift right here. There's no need to press on in God." So God moves on to Bethel and we stay in Gilgal.

Bethel means "the house of God" or "the God of the house." Hebrews 3:6 says that we are His house. So at Bethel, Elijah called upon Elisha to refocus his heart on the Giver and not the gift. Elisha seemed to be set on Elijah's gift, the mantle—a double portion. Well, Elijah knew this had to be tested or this young man with the double portion could go off in a very heady way unless there was order from God. There had to be a circumcision of his heart so his circumcised heart could be refocused more on the Giver than on the gifts.

From there they went to Jericho. Jericho, "the city of palms" or "the city of fragrance," the perfuming of the gift. Once our heart is circumcised and we have been exposed to God, then we can handle rightly the things God gives to us. We recognize this is the house of God. He is the God of this house, so we focus on Him rather than the gifts we desire to be empowered to express. It often becomes difficult at that point for that is when we begin experiencing the praises of men: "Boy that was a good word"; "Man, bless God for that"; "Wow, I've never seen anybody pray like that"; "You know, I've never seen anyone do what you did with so much anointing." It doesn't take long until our focus is directed off of the Giver and back to the gifts again.

Pride begins to rise up again as we think of how God has chosen us to be an honored and chosen vessel. We do a bit of "sanctified" strutting. We are a little too sophisticated to strut outwardly, so we do it in the secret place of the heart, where only we and God know exactly what is happening. Everyone else may seem impressed, but we can't fool God. A good question to ask ourselves at this point, as a reality check, is, "Am I bringing glory to God, or...am I merely impressive?"

Jericho is the place of the perfuming of the gift. A young man came to me saying, "I have been so destroyed by some leaders, could you talk to me? I need to talk." So I met with him. As we shared, he looked at me and said, "I don't know anyone who thinks like you do. I really mean it, I've never met anyone who thinks like you or teaches like you teach." You know, for a moment there I felt this thing inside of me rise up in pride to receive the accolades. Then I realized what was happening. My thinking processes came back into God's order as I reminded myself, "I am merely the carrier of what he is experiencing. Whatever it is he is noticing, it is God!" It is my privilege to be the vessel through whom God is expressed. The perfuming of your own gifts comes from the recognition of men. So, what God must do is test our gifts to see whether or not we can respond righteously to the praises of men.

False humility is as sinful as pride. It is reverse pride. It is worse than the outright boastful kind of pride because it's so subtle and so deceptive. We must learn to respond rightly to the praises of men, the perfuming of the gift. A right response is a simple "thank you." What else do you have to say? You don't have to present a religious sounding response. Just say, "thank you."

Elijah and Elisha

Are you willing to purchase the gift by the laying down of your mind, your emotions, and your will? Having been at Gilgal, the place of the circumcision of the heart, Elijah and Elisha went on to Bethel where they saw the house of God and the God of the house. After refocusing on the Giver, they proceeded to Jericho where Elijah taught Elisha how to respond righteously to the praises of men. Elisha passed the tests designed by Elijah so they continued on to Jordan. Jordan means "descending," descending into humility.

Promotion comes through humility. Just keep serving God and He will exalt you. However, if your concern is *when* the exaltation is coming, you can count on the fact that it will not come. The Father knows you aren't ready to handle it.

The mantle fell at the Jordan. Elijah went up in the whirlwind and the mantle fell. There was promotion for Elisha through the humility God worked into his life through Elijah. Having been through this process in which he kept serving God until God began to exalt him, Elisha took the mantle, smote the waters, and crossed over the Jordan again. This was not an act of pride. It was the initial demonstration of the double portion power of God that had been poured out upon him. He was being exalted and promoted through the humility. He recognized his place, and he was no longer going to misuse the gifts.

Elijah was removed. Just as there was the divine removal of Moses so Joshua could take over his ministry, there was also a divine removal of Elijah so Elisha could have a double portion of the gift and blessing of God. Not only do we find the truths of the spiritual father/son relationship in the Old Testament, the New Testament gives us examples as well. One such example is that of Paul and Timothy.

Chapter 14

Paul and Timothy

Paul imparted his heart to Timothy. In fact, the Scripture speaks of Paul and Timothy as having the same spirit.

For I have no one else of kindred spirit who will genuinely be concerned for your welfare. For they all seek after their own interests, not those of Christ Jesus. But you know of his proven worth that he served with me in the furtherance of the gospel like a child serving his father.
Philippians 2:20

Paul speaks of Timothy as possessing a kindred spirit with him.

Serving is doing whatever the father says has to be done. Paul says, "He served me in many ways." Timothy carried baggage. He did not say, "Bless God, I've been to seminary. What am I doing carrying luggage? Bless God, when I was in seminary I used to preach on the streets and people were saved. What am I doing carrying this man's baggage and tapes? Why am I setting up a table? What's going on here? I've got my own ministry." Timothy understood the process. This was his season of serving Paul.

Paul knew that Timothy would be concerned for the welfare of the Philippians because Paul had experienced Timothy's concern first hand. Timothy took on the role of the servant. His only question was, "What can I do to serve my spiritual father?" He willingly put himself to learning by serving.

The blessing of the spiritual father after the Old Testament pattern is continued in the New Testament. In First Timothy 4:14, Paul wrote, "Do not neglect the spiritual gift within you, which was bestowed upon you through prophetic utterance with the laying on of hands by the presbytery." It is so important to recognize and receive the blessing of the father. Paul laid his hands on Timothy and gave him his blessing.

A natural father should give blessing to his natural sons and daughters, just as a spiritual father should give the blessing of God to his spiritual sons and daughters. Bless them often! When each of my sons asked to be married to the girl of their dreams, my wife and I said, "We bless what God has done." We hugged them and blessed them. We were blessing the workings of God in their lives.

In that process of blessing, a son operates with confidence. There is no mystery about whether or not there is acceptance. The son understands there is acceptance. Little sons and daughters ought to receive on a continuing basis the laying on of the father's hand and the declaration of blessing. The father should declare, "I bless the intelligence God has given you. I bless the understanding that God has put in your heart. I bless the response that you have to the Word of God. I bless the honesty you demonstrate to your mother and me. I bless your gifting. I bless your skills."

This is speaking the blessing after the Old Testament pattern, which breaks the bondage on a child's heart who needs the acceptance and approval of his or her father.

Often children are put in bondage simply by not hearing blessing. We break the bondage that is upon their hearts and lives by speaking blessings. The same thing is true in the realm of the spirit. Father God speaks blessing to us all through His book the Bible. He says, "I bless you, I have called you saints and chosen ones, priests and kings." He blesses us over and over again by giving us leaders who love us—pastors, evangelists, teachers, and prophets who bless us with the Word of God. We continually receive the blessing of the hand of God on our lives.

Unfortunately, we are not very alert to the blessings of God on our lives. So He approaches closer to us by giving us spiritual fathers and mothers to be a little more intimate with us than the pastor: "I bless your understanding of the Word of God. I bless the revelation God just gave to you. I bless the gifting I see rising up in you. I bless your skill at that carpentry work. God encourage that carpentry work in him. God encourage that computer expertise in him. I bless that. I bless your management skills." With that kind of blessing after the Old Testament pattern we break the bondage that's on our sons and daughters in the Kingdom of God. We break the bondage of the fear of not being accepted. We build up confident people for the Kingdom of God, not arrogant but confident. They will move into their business settings and household settings with the confidence of God. Giving blessings bonds the sons and the fathers more tightly together. A son blessed, a daughter blessed, is more willing to enjoy serving the father. In the realm of the spirit, you *know* how that works between you and God. The more you are blessed by God, the more committed you are to serving Him.

As a spiritual father, Paul first prepared Timothy to go. Then he sent him. Philippians 2:19 explains, "But I hope in the Lord Jesus to send Timothy to you shortly, so that I also may be encouraged when I learn of your condition." Paul, the father, prepared Timothy to go, and then he sent him. One of the lessons a son must learn is that "just because I am invited, it does not mean I am sent." Someone may invite a son to minister in an honorable way or place, but that doesn't mean the son is ready to step out into such a ministry.

In my life as a pastor, I have leaders around me, who speak into my life. Every invitation I receive is talked over and prayed over with our elders, as well as my wife. I will not say "yes" until I know those around me support the decision. There have been times I have been invited to places of ministry that sounded wonderful, yet I could not accept. There is something about getting on an airplane and flying off to another city to bring the Word that causes you to feel as though you must be important. Yet, it is nothing. There have been times I have shared about an invitation with our elders and my wife, and they have warned me not to accept. God has given us wives and fathers in our lives to help us know the will of God.

When we have a dream or a vision in our hearts, sometimes we do not see as clearly as we should. We get so involved with the vision, we think we can accomplish everything simultaneously. I remember the first time the elders said "no" to me. I had shared with them an invitation that I thought for sure was going to be my big break. The elders said, "Paul we have prayed about this thing and you have taught us that just because you are called does not mean you are sent," so they told me "no." I chafed under that as I drove home frustrated. At home I shared with my wife who said, "Honey, I felt the same way. I told you I had a big check in my spirit that something would happen there that would not be in God's order for you." Our Father makes sure we have been prepared for a place before He sends us there. Paul sent Timothy with confidence to encourage them in the Lord.

Finally, in Acts 20:38, there was the divine removal of the apostle Paul out of Timothy's life, and he was released to express the heart of the apostle Paul, which was the heart of God in his own ministry. The heart is the center for our deepest, inner qualities that we will share with others in our lives and ministry.

We have found then that there are three types of spiritual fathering: Moses to Joshua, where the son inherits the ministry; Elijah to Elisha, where the son inherits the gift; and Paul to Timothy, where the son inherits the heart. Next, we will discover characteristics that will reveal maturity in our spiritual sons.

Part 5

Unleashing Mature Sons

You therefore, my son, be strong in the grace that is in Christ Jesus. And the things which you have heard from me in the presence of many witnesses, these entrust to faithful men, who will be able to teach others also. Suffer hardship with me, as a good soldier of Christ Jesus. No soldier in active service entangles himself in the affairs of everyday life, so that he may please the one who enlisted him as a soldier. And also, if anyone competes as an athlete, he does not win the prize unless he competes according to the rules. The hard-working farmer ought to be the first to receive his share of the crops. Consider what I say, for the Lord will give you understanding in everything.

2 Timothy 2:1-7

Chapter 15

Characteristics of a Mature Son

How does a spiritual father know when a son has reached a level of maturity that allows him to be released into ministry in the most powerful and effective way? Many things will vary from person to person. There is no established, objective test that will say one person is mature and another is not. Instead, we must evaluate every one of our spiritual children based on principles of maturity from the Word of God. I have discovered seven principles that represent a mature son, and I share them here as a means of helping to guide the spiritual father in releasing his son.

Representation Rather Than Substitution

The first principle is that the mature son must know his responsibility is to represent his father rather than substitute for him. Hebrews 1:3 reads, "And [Jesus] is the radiance of God's glory and the exact representation of His [God's] nature, and upholds all things by the word of His power." A mature son understands that he represents instead of substitutes.

The word meaning "to represent" actually means "to stand on behalf of the original so as to not displace the original." What did Jesus do when the Pharisees criticized Him about His life and ministry? He explained that He was only speaking what the Father had given Him to speak (see Jn. 12:49). Jesus never set Himself above His Father in His own mind or in the presence of others. Just as the natural son understands that he represents the father, so the spiritual son represents his spiritual father. He is not a substitute for the father.

When a son believes he is a substitute and that he will go take the place of his father, he draws to himself the loyal subjects of his father. Absalom is a good example. He stood in the gate and said, "Now this problem you have, the way my father will handle it is this way, but if *I* were the king, I'd handle it like this." The people responded, "Wow, we like the way you do it better, so let's make you king." (See Second Samuel 15:1-6.) You see, the son who begins to take his gifting into his own hands and move about presenting it before it is ready to be presented is attempting to be a substitute for his father rather than a representative of him.

Representing the father as Jesus does means to stand on behalf of the original so as to not displace the original. This works in sonship and daughtership in the Church of Jesus Christ. Where people are part of a church family, they must understand that the father of the house, the senior pastor, the set man, the leader of that church, has been put there to lead by God. There are those with big gifts who will come into the place of ministry. The father demonstrates the largeness of the heart of God by openly receiving those who have equal or stronger gifts than his own. Those who have equal or stronger gifts than the father of

Characteristics of a Mature Son

the house demonstrate their sonship by keeping their gift under the integrity and supervision of the leadership of that house.

However, there are those who believe their gifts are bigger than the leadership of the house, and they will draw others to themselves as they take on the role of substituting for the father rather than representing him. Churches often have spiritual fathers, elders of the house, who are genuine, warm, compassionate, loving, and gentle-hearted men. Perhaps the pastor has a prophetic gifting and as such demonstrates a harsh edge in his personality. People may love him dearly, but there may be times they are almost afraid of him. A bit unwilling to get too close for fear of being wounded and offended, they back away from him. Regardless of their efforts he wounds and hurts them, so they speak to a loving elder. If that loving elder does not know he represents the father of the house, he may, by his demeanor, innuendoes, body language, over indulgence, and compassionate response, draw them to himself as a substitute. He may feel the necessity to excuse the father of the house. In the process of making excuses for him, the elder may be so caring and understanding that he draws that person (or persons) to himself. The sons must remember they represent, not substitute for, the father. In this case the son must lead the wounded person to the father of the house to deal righteously with the situation. In this way the son remains a representative.

The effort to substitute often leads to splits in the house of Jesus Christ. There will be no grace for that leader, whether it is an elder or a home group leader, to father other people because he is not yet in the fathering season of his life. They have been called to the house to be an elder, not a shepherd-father, so grace for that ministry will elude him.

There are so many men who have large gifts of benevolence, grace, compassion, and mercy. And when a pastor speaks the word with authority, the wounded heart says, "Oh, he's so hard, he draws such a firm line, there doesn't seem to be any leeway in his teaching at all. He seems so inflexible; his preaching is toxic. I come to church to be blessed and encouraged, and I go away with the word that speaks about obedience—again. I know all about obedience." A mature son understands he represents the father of the house. So he will use his big gifts to stand with the father as his representative in the house, giving understanding and encouragement to the wounded ones without impuning the character of his father. If the elder or leader is concerned about his father's ways, he will appeal to him about it in private.

Lover of Discipline

The mature son loves the father's discipline. The writer of Hebrews teaches:

> *You have not yet resisted to the point of shedding blood in your striving against sin; and you have forgotten the exhortation which is addressed to you as sons, "My son, do not regard lightly the discipline of the Lord, nor faint when you are reproved by Him; for those whom the Lord loves He disciplines, and He scourges every son whom He receives."*
>
> Hebrews 12:4-6

The mature son loves the discipline of his father. He is not angry at discipline; he loves discipline.

Discipline of the spiritual father, just like discipline of our Father God, is not angry discipline. It is loving discipline. One of the things that we Americans need to learn in the Church of Christ is we have bought the world's understanding of how to confront and deal with conflict. That is why there is so much disturbance in the Church of Jesus Christ. We don't understand how to deal with conflict in our marriages, and we don't understand how to deal with conflict in personal relationships because we don't know how to righteously confront one another. It seems that we only understand the world's pattern, which includes working up a good level of frustration over a considerable period of time. Too often this leads to saying things in an attitude and tone of voice that are as sinful as the issue we desire to confront.

Here is another "Americanism": We don't ask forgiveness, we just say "sorry about that." You see, the difference between being sorry and asking forgiveness is forgiveness admits guilt, "I did that to you. I ask you to forgive me. Please." Teens often complain to me about their parents. My response is, "If you had to tell me a percentage, 100 percent being how much someone is wrong, in dealing with you, would you say your parents are 98 percent wrong?"

"Yeah, at least."

"Okay, your parents are 98 percent wrong in dealing with you. Are you wrong the other 2 percent?"

"Yeah, probably."

"Then the Word of God says you need to repent for that 2 percent of error like it was 100 percent. Ask your parents to forgive you for sinning against them. Let God turn their hearts toward you.

Often, we ask forgiveness like this, "You know, I'm going to ask you to forgive me because I responded so poorly when you hurt me so badly. I was destroyed by it, so I ask you to forgive me." We want to make sure they understand they are responsible. But that is God's responsibility to teach them. Our responsibility is to say, "I ask you to forgive me for this response and this attitude. It is ungodly. Will you forgive me?" We must not limit our responsibility to a portion of the problem. We must recognize that *our* involvement is sinful so true forgiveness can be received. Repentance says, "I am guilty" period. We can hardly wait to let them know how poorly they *made* us respond to them, and that it was their fault we acted in an ungodly manner. No! God says you have a responsibility to be righteous regardless of what someone else does. The son loves the loving discipline of the father.

We learn how to confront and deal with conflict righteously by responding as the Father does to you and me. The Father says, "This is the way, walk in it" (see Is. 30:21). Then He lets you choose to obey or disobey (see Is. 30:21). He does not make you do it. The Father gives loving discipline. If we respond to it, we benefit from it. If we resist it, He has to give a little more firm discipline. The spiritual father speaks and the son is not offended because he understands the role of his father, his spiritual father, in helping him become a man of God. He has a mature understanding about his father's role in his life. Now he not only waits for the loving discipline, he asks for it. The son that waits for his natural father to give him discipline is hoping his father has not noticed he needs it. But the mature son recognizes the need for the father's discipline. He desires his father to lead him by giving it.

One Under Authority

The mature son walks well under authority.

Now I say, as long as the heir is a child, he does not differ at all from a slave although he is owner of everything, but he is under guardians and managers until the date set by the father.
Galatians 4:1-2

Let me see if I can say this so that it is clear. You will never be given more authority than you are willing to yield to. You will never be given more authority than you demonstrate a willingness to be under.

What made the centurion an example of great faith to Jesus was the fact the centurion knew by experience what it meant to be under authority (see Mt. 8:5-13). Having demonstrated a willingness to yield and to be under authority the centurion had been given a great deal of authority. In the measure of the authority he lived under, he was given authority over others. It is a principle of the Kingdom of God that when I have lived under authority I will be given the same measure of authority.

A mature son walks well under authority. He understands that he will not be given any more authority than he has been willing to walk under. He understands the timing of the father. There is a date set by the father (see

Gal. 4:2). Notice that phrase, "until the date set by the father." You will be under guardians and managers until the date set by the father. In spiritual fathering, as well as in natural fathering, the father understands the heart of God for his son. The relationship of the son to his (natural or spiritual) father helps him understand he is not ready until the date set by the father. It is still a hard thing for a son to wait for the time for his release.

Faithful in Another's Field

The mature son labors faithfully in the field of another. In the story of the unrighteous steward we find,

> *If therefore you have not been faithful in the use of unrighteous mammon, who will entrust the true riches to you? And if you have not been faithful in the use of that which is another's, who will give you that which is your own? No servant can serve two masters; for either he will hate the one, and love the other, or else he will hold to the one, and despise the other. You cannot serve God and mammon.*
>
> Luke 16:11-13

The Word says our Father God cannot trust us with any more riches than we have already demonstrated an ability to care for through His riches so freely given to us. In other words, when I demonstrate I can properly steward natural riches, He will trust me with a greater proportion of spiritual riches.

The story of the prodigal son speaks of two sons who squandered the inheritance of their father. (See Luke 15:13-32.) You know the story of the prodigal who went off and squandered all his wealth while the other son stayed home. Yet there is also a problem with the elder son who stayed home. He had an ungodly attitude. He did not have an attitude of gratitude and faithful servanthood while he toiled in the field of his father. His attitude was, "I will serve in the field of my father until the old guy croaks, and then it will all be mine." The righteous son labors faithfully in the field of another man knowing that his entire labor will bring him nothing more than the recognition that he has served, that's all.

> *But which of you, having a slave plowing or tending sheep, will say to him when he has come in from the field, "Come immediately and sit down to eat"? But will he not say to him, "Prepare something for me to eat, and properly clothe yourself and serve me until I have eaten and drunk; and afterward you will eat and drink"? He does not thank the slave because he did the things which were commanded, does he? So you too, when you do all the things which are commanded you, say, "We are unworthy slaves; we have done only that which we ought to have done."*
>
> Luke 17:7-10

There is a necessity on the part of the father to express appreciation for a job well done. It is important for a father to bless his son's efforts at obedience and servanthood. But the child has to learn, just as a spiritual son must learn, he has only done what he ought to have done. It wasn't anything out of the ordinary. It was no big deal. Being asked to do a task and doing that task beyond what was requested are two different things. If we have only done what we have been asked to do, though recognition may be given it is not required. But the mature son who labors faithfully in the field of another does not need recognition because his commitment is to excellent servanthood, without acknowledgement. His commitment to excellence in his father's name is to serve the task to completion, and while he is at it, doing other tasks with that same excellence without being asked. He serves in the field of another with faithfulness and gladness of heart.

Led by the Spirit

A mature son is led by the Holy Spirit. Romans 8:14 reads, "For all who are being led by the Spirit of God, these are sons of God." He is led by the Spirit of God, so when he receives instruction from the Spirit of God in his private closet, what does he do? Does he come out of the closet and march off on his own? No! He marches straight to his father and says, "God spoke to me. I really believe He said this. Can you help me with that? What do you hear in this? What do you see in this?" The father has the privilege to give his blessing to his son who has an ear to hear the leading of the Spirit of God. He blesses the hearing and the leading of the spirit in the son, which encourages the son to keep hearing the leadership of the Spirit of God.

Set to Receive

The mature son can fully receive and benefit from the inheritance he will receive. In other words, he is postured to receive his inheritance. Through all of the experiences of the seasons of life, the son becomes prepared to receive from God.

And because you are sons, God has sent forth the Spirit of His Son into our hearts, crying, "Abba!

Characteristics of a Mature Son

Father!" Therefore you are no longer a slave, but a son; and if a son, then an heir through God.
                                    Galatians 4:6-7

A mature son can fully receive and benefit from his inheritance; he is postured to receive it.

What postures him to receive the inheritance is that he has been walking in obedience. He has been walking in servanthood. He has been walking through the seasons of his life understanding the wisdom of God in preparing him for leadership. He has been walking in the timing of God, which postures him to receive the inheritance. So many spiritual sons long to receive the inheritance of God, but they are not postured to receive. Perhaps they have been resistant to authority. Or they may have been resistant to the leadership God has put over them as an individual or to the spiritual leadership God places in the house. They may think it is time their gift should come forth, but they are not postured to receive the inheritance of the full expression of the gift.

The son who has been faithful, who represents rather than substitutes, who loves discipline, who walks under authority, who labors faithfully in the field of another—he is postured to receive his inheritance. He is led by the Spirit of God under his appointed authority, so he is postured to receive his inheritance of coming forth in the full responsibility and expression of his gift.

The Son Is Not a Slave

The mature son is not a slave, but he is a freed man. "Therefore you are no longer a slave, but a son; and if a son, then an heir through God" (Gal. 4:7). The mature son is a freed son. A slave has areas of his heart that are still bondage within him. The son has been freed from bondage, having pressed through the seasons of God. Now those areas are experiencing the liberty of God. You see, his relationship to his spiritual father has taught him the pain and pleasure of these qualities: of being pressed and broken as a representative, of loving the father's discipline, of walking well under the father's authority, of laboring faithfully in the father's household, and of listening to and learning how to respond to the leading of the Holy Spirit.

He is fully postured to receive his inheritance, and he is a freed man. He no longer has the bondages in him. He no longer has the desire to burst out on his own and run like a stallion. He now knows when the corral has opened and the Master, the Father God, is sitting in the saddle with His hands on the reins as He sends him to a specific place of leadership. Mature sons proceed with direction, purpose, and destiny to fulfill that assignment under the banner of the Kingdom of God, under the fullness of the righteousness of God in his heart.

The mature son is ready to be unleashed. The spiritual father must let go of the bridle and allow the son to step out and take his position of leadership in the Kingdom of God. Unleashing sons and daughters of the Kingdom who have been blessed and prospered through their seasons of life will bring about an anointing and revival for future generations.

Chapter 16

Unleashing Sons With Power

The apostle Paul understood about letting go of a son. In the Book of Second Timothy he gave final instructions to his spiritual son as he unleashed Timothy to leadership on his own.

You therefore, my son, be strong in the grace that is in Christ Jesus. And the things which you have heard from me...these entrust to faithful men, who will be able to teach others also.
2 Timothy 2:1-2

You, however, continue in the things you have learned and become convinced of, knowing from whom you have learned them; and that from childhood you have known the sacred writings which are able to give you the wisdom that leads to salvation through faith which is in Christ Jesus.
2 Timothy 3:14

Two Keys

In the Church, we release people to leadership depending upon their education or their giftings. These may be helpful, but God's keys are *heart* and *character*. It appears God is more concerned with simplicity and purity of devotion to Jesus than He is with our education or giftings.

This is illustrated in Paul's final instructions to Timothy. (See Second Timothy 2.)

...be strong in Grace
...endure hardship
...not entangled with affairs of everyday life
...avoid worldly and empty chatter
...flee youthful lusts
...hold a high standard in faith and love
...be sincere.

Paul desired Timothy to be released with the power of a life that demonstrates the heart and character of Jesus.

Released With Power

Too often the word *power* is interpreted to mean the expressions of the so-called "power-gifts"—healing, miracles, and prophecy. Since Jesus is our example, let us observe His ministry with power. You will recall that the Pharisees were more concerned with who Jesus was than about what He did. Although they challenged His actions on a few occasions, it was His claims to sonship with the Father that prompted their greatest wrath. Jesus Himself said it was His relationship with the Father that enabled Him to do the works He did.

Why should it be different for us? It appears there is only one reason that we desire ministering in the gifts before our heart relationship with God has prepared us to do so: It is man's way to desire an honored reputation above his relationship with the Father. Jesus' life style of power was established through His relationship with the Father. His heart and character reflected Their intimacy.

His ministry of "power-gifts" authenticated His life, and His life authenticated His gifts.

A spiritual father is delighted to release his sons to leadership in the Church because he knows the power they possess has first been demonstrated in the heart and character of Jesus within them. The sons' giftings will flow easily with the double-portion anointing because of their intimacy with God.

Aware of the Times

> *But realize this, that in the last days difficult times will come.*
>
> 2 Timothy 3:1

As Timothy was released, Paul gave him a realistic awareness of what he would face in the Church.

> *For men will be lovers of self, lovers of money, boastful, arrogant, revilers, disobedient to parents, ungrateful, unholy, unloving, irreconcilable, malicious gossips, without self-control, brutal, haters of good, treacherous, reckless, conceited, lovers of pleasure rather than lovers of God; holding to a form of godliness, although they have denied its power... oppose[rs of] truth, men of depraved mind, rejected as regards the faith. ...evil men and imposters will proceed from bad to worse, deceiving and being deceived.*
>
> 2 Timothy 3:2-13

The sons we release to lead the church to its destiny and final glory will face all of this and more in increased measure. They will be required to be as the sons of Issachar.

And of the sons of Issachar, men who understood the times, with knowledge of what [the people of God] *should do....*
                                    1 Chronicles 12:32

That is why God has ordained the powerful ministry of spiritual fatherhood. It is our privilege to prepare our sons to endure the hardness and persecution that comes to "all who desire to live godly in Christ Jesus" (2 Tim. 3:12).

Our sons' release with the power of intimate relationship with the Father assures us of their awareness of the times and of their preparation to be overcomers. These sons have an advantage. Spiritual fathers will prepare this next generation to be a new breed of leaders who have a maturity that has been born out of submission, obedience, responsibility, and accountability. They will have unwavering maturity beyond their years, developed in the crucible of sonship where they learned:

H—humility
E—endurance
R—repentance
O—obedience

Yes, these sons and daughters will be ready to meet the challenges of this new age because they will be God's new breed of leaders.

A New Breed

The demands of an ever increasing sin-sick Church and world will require a new breed of leaders. They will be prepared to face it without fear because they will have learned from their fathers that the fear of man leads to the ultimate bondage, but the fear of the Lord releases them to the ultimate freedom.

With few exceptions, previous generations have not experienced this kind of preparation for leadership in the Church. But God is awakening the fathers and mothers in the house of God to the awesome resources stored up in the lives of the young men and women in our churches. Sons and daughters are being chosen and the preparations through the seasons of life are beginning.

This new breed of leaders of the Church will be distinctly different from the leaders the Church has tolerated in the past. Because of the fathering they will receive, their intimate relationship with the Father will cause their double-portion life style of power to release their double-portion gifting of power in larger measure than we have ever seen or experienced.

No All-Stars

There will be no concern among these new leaders about who gets recognized as *the* leader. What their fathers taught them about humility, submissiveness, and accountability will prepare them to take their place in the Kingdom of God. They will care only that Jesus Christ is glorified. Selfish ambition will not reign among this new breed of leaders. Maintaining large ministries and reputations will be of no concern to them. Their hearts and character, having been tried and proven, will keep them from falling prey to the temptations the "great" independent leaders of this generation have experienced. They will be delighted if no one knows who they are or what great things they can do in Jesus' name, because their commitment will be to Jesus and one another. Preferring and loving one another will demonstrate they have learned to be truly interdependent.

Petty preferences and prejudice will melt away as they become reconcilers in the Church. They will follow the example of their intimate lover and friend Jesus, and they will become initiators in the ministry of reconciliation. They will pay the price, perhaps of persecution, for teaching and modeling that the true Church of Jesus is integrated, crossing every imaginable preconceived preference and prejudice.

This is the Church our spiritual sons and daughters will lead, a powerful, glorious Church. It is His Bride, which is being beautified in preparation for the coming of the groom—the King, Jesus Christ the Lord. Imagine its power and influence in the earth. I want to live to see it happen.

For us to see it happen, there must arise in the Church today spiritual fathers and mothers who will lay down their lives to raise up this new breed of leaders for the Church of Jesus Christ.

Is There a Father in the House?